ENDO.

You will not be able to put this book down! This is a really great book on how to open the sometimes-unseen world of Angels from the Lord. Keith shares some powerful stories and exercises that will activate you to a new level. Keith gives some pointers for helping children and dives deeper into what the Bible says about angels and the supernatural.

DOUG ADDISON
Doug Addison.com
Author of Hearing God Everyday, Daily Prophetic Words,
Spirit Connection Webcast, Podcast and Prophetic Blog.

Keith provides a balanced biblical approach to partnering with angels that anyone can relate to and follow. His personal stories are helpful and enlightening in revealing the ways that we are already interacting with the angelic realm. The biblical examples and main points carve a path for developing deeper understanding of angels while keeping the focus clearly on God's person, character, and purposes.

DAN MCCOLLAM
Founder of The Prophetic Company and
co-founder Bethel School of the Prophet

Keith is probably one of the most relevent voices and prophets of the hour!!! I have known Keith since he was a small town pastor in Willits California some twenty plus years ago. I've watched his growth and influence explode since becoming a part of the team in Vacaville at the mission to where he is literally influencing the world thru his emerging prophets school. When you read this book it will inspire and equip you to move to a new level in the kingdom and the prophetic and will help to position you for the greatest hour to be alive!!!!!! I look forward to seeing whats next in Keith's life and I declare a blessing on those who read this book.

WENDELL MCGOWAN
Wendell McGowan Ministries, Las Vegas, Nevada

Keith has written a timely and significant resource for the body of Christ. This book will help you see the Biblical protocols for interacting and partnering with the angelic and how this understanding can yield Kingdom results. Tools such as this are so vital for the Kingdom to continue to be advanced in an efficient and powerful way.

BRIAN ORM
Co-Founder of Kingdomstrate, Author of Jumpstart, Little Beans and
a Big God, The Ascended Life, and Remember When

© Copyright 2019—Keith Ferrante

All rights reserved. This book is protected by the copyright laws of the United States of America. This book may not be copied or reprinted for commercial gain or profit. The use of short quotations or occasional page copying for personal or group study is permitted. Unless otherwise identified, Scripture quotations are taken from the HOLY BIBLE, NEW INTERNATIONAL VERSION®. Copyright © 1973, 1978, 1984 International Bible Society. Used by permission of Zondervan. All rights reserved. Scripture quotations marked "NKJV" are taken from the HOLY BIBLE, NEW KING JAMES VERSION®. Copyright © 1982 by Thomas Nelson, Inc. Used by permission. All rights reserved. Scripture quotations marked "KJV" are taken from the KING JAMES VERSION (KJV): KING JAMES VERSION, public domain. Scripture quotations marked "MSG" are taken from The Message. Copyright © 1993, 1994, 1995, 1996, 2000, 2001, 2002. Used by permission of NavPress Publishing Group. www.navpress.com.

Published by *Emerging Prophets*
Contact *admin@emergingprophets.com, EmergingProphets.com*
Cover design *Franziska Haase / @coverdungeonrabbit*
Editing *Heather Nunn*
Interior Layout *Olivier Darbonville*

Printed in the United States of America

A PRACTICAL GUIDE TO
Partnering
—— with ——
Angels

KEITH FERRANTE

Contents

Introduction **7**

ONE / Embrace That You Can See Angels **11**

TWO / Engaging the Angelic Realm **21**

THREE / Touching the Angelic Realm **31**

FOUR / Finding Angels **39**

FIVE / Everyone Can See Angels **47**

SIX / What is Your Name Mr. Angel? **55**

SEVEN / Different Kinds of Angels **61**

EIGHT / Partnering With the Angelic **69**

NINE / Angelic Activity **77**

TEN / Testing the Angelic Realm **85**

ELEVEN / Angels That Help Us **93**

TWELVE / Differing Authority in the Angelic **99**

THIRTEEN / Partnering With the Angelic Unleashes Provision **105**

FOURTEEN / Angels Honor God's Value **111**

INTRODUCTION

It was over fifteen years ago when I first remember being ministered to by angels. My wife, Heather, and I had been leading worship for a family camp that had brought in hundreds of people. We had led worship about thirteen different times and were worn out. In that season, we were contending for revival in a region that was having mixed feelings about the revival. There were several people in the churches of the region that were for the revival and a number that were against. I had also been against the revival until I encountered God in that same camp a couple of years before. Now I was the one helping to push for that same move of God to come into the earth but there was resistance. Some of the leaders at the camp, including the main speakers, weren't happy with the revival or those who represented it in any measure. Heather and I and our worship band were part of that group that now represented revival.

Every worship service we led was met with some kind of resistance. Every time we finished the worship set we would be called aside and asked to change something for the next worship set. Each time we changed, trying our best to honor the leaders, God would still show up. By the end of the thirteen sets, the leaders were sitting on the front row of the meeting with their arms crossed, eyes glaring, and hearts closed to what we were doing. We weren't doing anything evil, we were simply pressing in for more of God during the worship times. Eventually, the resistance from the opposing leaders had worn us out.

Heather and I went to bed that night and to our wonderful surprise, we both began to simultaneously feel the presence of God through an angelic encounter. It was like nothing we had ever experienced. We began to feel waves of His presence come up and down our bodies from the top of our heads to the soles of our feet. At first, it started in our feet and then worked its way up and then back down again. It was amazing. What was even more amazing was that it was happening to both of us at the same time. As we lay in bed we asked each other if we were feeling the same thing, the presence of God through ministering angels. I don't know how we knew it was angels. We weren't experienced in knowing the difference between the angelic and the Lord but somehow we knew. Of course, the angels were there to administer the presence of the Lord. So, technically it was both. But we both sensed angels were ministering to us in that room.

The wonderful fruit of that encounter was that our hearts were filled with love again and restored from the exhausting week of leading morning and night session worship where we had experienced such resistance. The next morning we both woke up revived. I was so revived I went and saw the main speaker, who was resistant to this revival; the revival of the presence, power, and love of God. I asked him if I could pray for him before I had to leave to go back home to the church I pastored at the time. He allowed me to pray for him and when I did the presence of God really touched him. I'm certain it was a byproduct of the angelic encounter we had experienced the night before. I had a love for this man even though he had been resisting what we were pursuing through worship. That love had come from the

INTRODUCTION

encounter the night before. After I was finished praying, he said, "Wow, I felt the anointing as you prayed." That prayer so impacted him that he spoke later that night about the encounter. He actually mentioned us in the message and the anointing he felt through the prayer; even though he hadn't been too sure about our revival methods. God works in mysterious ways and angels are often agents to release those wonderful mysteries.

A few years back, I received a prophecy from a powerful prophetic voice stating that Heather and I would be taken into a season where we would learn the ministry of angels. I thought that was exciting but it did seem rather far out from what I had confidence for. That prophecy stated that we would need to learn to partner with the angels for a greater breakthrough. These last few years have been just that, a wonderful journey of encountering angels and learning how to partner with them to see greater Kingdom breakthrough.

My hope in writing this book is that you will grow in faith that you too can encounter and partner with angels just like I have learned to do. To some, it may seem off-limits to encounter and talk with angels. I hope to demystify some wrong beliefs you may have about interacting with angels. I believe this book will be a guide in teaching you how to partner with angels. I have read many books on angels that have a lot of great content in them. I love that people are writing about the angelic and the supernatural. At times, some of these books can come across as impersonal, informational, or perhaps have such lofty stories that we would never hope to attain. I appreciate and highly value the stories of the prophets and others that give us an example to follow but I don't want to feel like what they have encountered is out of reach. Prophets often seem to be the ones sharing about angelic encounters. I know others can as well but if a prophet shares the prophet's job is to equip the saints. So if you see something in the life of a prophet it should be an invitation for the Body of Christ to step into that. For too long it has felt like there's a huge gap between what the prophet experiences and what the saints experience. My hope in writing this book is that you will be inspired to step into that spiritual realm to discover the wonderful mysteries God has given to His children and that He wants you to enjoy. I want you to come away from reading this book with a revelation that you are meant to encounter the spiritual realm and it isn't something to be afraid of. It isn't an impersonal realm. It is the realm of a good Father God. You simply need to understand the parameters God designed for His Bride to walk in within this realm, learn how to plunge into the depths of glory, and fly into the heights of heavenly encounters that are waiting for you.

May your eyes be opened as you read this book and may you realize that you were meant to encounter and partner with the angels. Understanding how to do that may give you the edge you have needed to see the breakthroughs to the promises of God you have been contending for. Just like Paul's prayer in Ephesians 1, my prayer for you is that the eyes of your heart would be enlightened that you may know Him better. And as you read this book, let your hunger for the angelic realm be increased so that you encounter all God has stored up for you to embrace!

Much grace on your adventures in the angelic realm!

Keith Ferrante

CHAPTER ONE

EMBRACE THAT YOU CAN SEE ANGELS

Years ago as my spiritual understanding began to grow, I realized that I was actually seeing and hearing things in the spirit realm, not just in the physical realm, and had been for a very long time. The spirit realm was never talked about, so I had no one to validate that what I was seeing was acceptable to see and I certainly didn't ask anyone about it. On top of that, I didn't really know what I was seeing and had internally chalked up most of it as demonic. For some reason that was the only grid I had for what I could see in the spirit.

Many times I would be walking down the road at night and sense someone walking behind me. Whenever I would turn around to see who it was, there would be no one there. Other times I would be in the church building and sense a presence nearby. I would see a shadow in the corner of the room and always assumed it was demonic. For some reason, I was always afraid when I sensed those things around me. I didn't know what was going on and I never verbalized it either. I wonder how many others out there have had experiences with the spirit realm but have never verbalized it; they've just buried it deep within themselves? I did the same. I buried what I was experiencing, even though the encounters didn't stop.

It wasn't until I met a prophet in the late '90s named Wendell McGowan that I began to get a revelation that what I was seeing all along was the spirit realm. I had been seeing flashes of light as well as shadows in corners of rooms for a while. I thought the flashes were just coincidental, lights from a car driving by, or my eyes catching the glare of a lamp somewhere in the room. But the interesting thing was that these flashes kept occurring. I would also see shadows in the room or oftentimes feel a presence around me but had no idea what I was seeing in the spirit realm and certainly didn't know what to do with any of it.

I remember reading a book by Frank Peretti called, *This Present Darkness*. There was a passage in the book that talked about a young pastor who prayed and then two angels came to visit him as he prayed. I had a moment where I realized that this could be a picture of me. I thought, 'yes, this is me', but because I had grown up thinking these shadows were evil, I didn't pay enough attention to them to realize they were angels. I think whenever I felt them, because I assumed they were evil, it reinforced the stronghold of fear that I had in my life. I didn't feel protected, I often felt scared and alone. But then I met Wendell.

A PROPHET ENTERS

Wendell came into my life as I was just beginning to embrace the new move of God in the early '90s. I had gone to a meeting at Bethel Church in

Redding, CA, and a lady that I knew told me she wanted to have someone pray for me. I said anyone but that guy over there. I didn't know his name, but it was Wendell. He was powerful, full of fire, and scary to me. He was a prophet and mostly what I knew about prophets back then was that they would spot your sins and possibly call down the fire of judgment on you. Against my wishes, she brought Wendell over to me. He immediately began to prophesy things about me that he could never have known. He also began to describe me to a T. He said that I was a man of the Word and skittish of the new things that I was seeing in the spirit but that God would show me what I was seeing was in the Bible and it was Him. He did an unusual thing after that; usual for prophets but unusual to me. He blew on my stomach. Little did I know that as he blew on my stomach, he was placing a target on me for the angelic.

That night, my wife and I slept at my parents' house, who lived and pastored in the Anderson area near Redding. In the middle of the night, I awoke suddenly to the sound of wind in my room. There was a whirlwind whipping around in my room, what was going on? There was no wind outside as the night was calm but somehow inside my room, there was a wind. I sat up from my bed and began to prophesy. Prophecy was new to me but somehow at this moment, it was being activated in me. I knew this was connected to Wendell blowing on me earlier during the prayer session. My wife woke up a bit startled and declared, "Keith, you're prophesying!" It was a moment to remember for sure! There I was prophesying as an angelic wind whirled around us stirring up my prophetic gift.

The next morning my Dad asked me what the sound was that he'd heard in our room the night before. The whole thing perplexed me and when I saw Wendell the next day I told him what had happened. He said, "Keith, you just had a similar experience like Samuel had while in the house of Eli. You had an experience that your Father validated, just like Eli validated that Samuel was hearing the voice of the Lord. God was stirring up the prophetic in you through an angelic encounter." I thought, "Wow, really God?! That's so amazing and cool!"

Wendell became, and still is, an amazing father who has mentored me in the things of the Spirit as well as been like Samuel was to David, a mentor and a great encourager. I certainly wouldn't be where I am at today without his faithful mentorship.

As I began to get to know Wendell, I started asking him a lot of questions about the spirit realm. I was like a young hungry son who would follow him around every time I saw him. I would stand around him when he prophesied over people and would be the person that would stand behind the person he was prophesying over just in case they fell down under the power of the Spirit. I would catch them and help them fall to the ground without hurting themselves. I was receiving impartation and growing so much as I got around people like Wendell and other prophets who started coming into my life as well.

WHAT ABOUT THE SHADOWS AND FLASHES OF LIGHT?

One day I asked Wendell about the shadows and flashes of light I was seeing. I shared how I thought the shadows were demonic and the lights were my imagination. He said, "Keith, the demons mostly try to hide from you. They only show their faces when they are trying to intimidate you. The shadows you are seeing are the angelic." He also shared that if I verified that the lights weren't light from a car flashing on your wall then they really were the angelic. WOW! I was rocked. First of all, the revelation that I wasn't always seeing demons was so incredibly comforting. Finally being able to get answers for what was going on with me surrounding the unseen things was powerfully freeing. That one revelation set me free from so much fear. I awoke to the revelation that I didn't have to be afraid of the shadows. I could embrace the fact that there were angels around me, that they were for me, and that they were sent from the Father. I didn't have to fear. I also realized that seeing these flashes, shadows, etc. was just a starting point for me seeing in the spirit realm. The bottom line was that not only could I see, but I was also seeing.

Wendell has helped me get free of lots of fears over the years. He became a mentor that helped me grow in understanding what God was doing in my life in the supernatural realm. That it was a realm that was meant for me and that I didn't have to be afraid of it. Everything I saw and encountered I had always equated to the demonic realm. I had grown up with the belief that in the last days the very elect could very well be deceived. That fearful teaching had placed in me a fear of anything that I didn't understand and a belief that most anything in the supernatural realm was bad. The supernatural realm was dark and scary. Oddly, there wasn't an embracing of the supernatural realm. I mean after all, God is supernatural. But the primary stories I heard growing up in the Church were about demons, deception, and evil. I needed a spiritual detox and a renewed mind. Thoughts like what Wendell shared with me about the shadows being angels began to help me renew my mind and embrace the fact that God was for me, angels were around me, and demons were not primarily what I was seeing.

Now, I'm not discounting that some people legitimately see the demonic realm on a normal basis and that is a real part of it. I just know I needed a change in how I was thinking. I was bound by the fear of the demonic realm not because I was seeing it but because my beliefs had relegated most supernatural things to only the demonic realm.

Do you have a similar journey like me? Have you had experiences that you didn't have language or spiritual paradigm for? Have you not known what to do with what you see and feel in the spirit realm and so you have a fear in your life around the supernatural realm? Do you live in fear when you go places because you see and feel things? Do your unhealthy biblical views cause you to relegate everything in the unseen realm to the demonic realm? Like I said before, I know there is a very real demonic realm and many do see demons but I'm not specifically focusing on that in this book.

You may have similar experiences like me where you have been seeing things in the spirit such as flashes of light, shadows in the corner of a room, or even a sense of someone right behind you. Maybe you have been aware of these things for years but you haven't known what they are. Maybe you have thought you were a bit crazy or weird. Maybe you shared with others about what you have experienced or felt and they were not helpful, perhaps judged you, told you those things weren't real or told you to get deliverance.

Yes, there is a place for deliverance. But deliverance is not needed just because you see, hear, or feel things in the spirit realm. Deliverance is needed because a spirit of fear was allowed into your life. Sometimes we need prayer to get rid of the demonic footholds in our life. Other times we simply need the revelation that we are seeing something and there is nothing wrong with us. Maybe like me, you need a revelation of truth; that what you are seeing isn't always the demonic. You may need to realize that there are things you see and feel in rooms wherever you go that are good things; they're God's agents.

FIRST STEPS

I think one of the first steps for us to be able to see into the spirit realm and operate in it at the level God has designed for us, is to get free of any fear related to seeing in the spirit. We need a revelation that we can see angels and what God is doing, and not everything supernatural is relegated to the demonic realm. Why is this revelation so important? Because, like me, I had a belief growing up that the very elect could be deceived. I had a fear of being deceived. This fear was causing me to see everything from a fear perspective instead of trusting God's goodness. That fear led me to believe everything was potentially bad. I needed a change of perspective. I needed to realize that I had such a good Daddy. I didn't realize that if I asked for bread, He wouldn't give me a snake.

> *"Which of you, if his son asks for bread, will give him a stone? Or if he asks for a fish, will give him a snake? If you, then, though you are evil, know how to give good gifts to your children, how much more will your Father in heaven give good gifts to those who ask Him!"*
>
> Matthew 7:9-11

He's such a good Father. I needed to stop fearing that I would be deceived. The words Wendell spoke over me helped start the process of freedom from the fear of being deceived. I was then able to start embracing that angels were around, that I was protected, I wasn't on my own, and I wasn't always being watched by demons. I had such fear in this realm but God was starting to free me of the fear. Now I could embrace the angelic, the supernatural, the spirit realm and learn more about the realm my Daddy lives in. My God is after all firstly, a Spirit, the Spirit of the living God. If you have fear of being deceived you will never even start to enter into heavenly encounters. They may be happening to you but they won't accelerate until you begin to embrace what they are. Yes, there is a place to discern good and evil and to learn what is God and what is not. That is for another book. But for now, let's just embrace that the angelic realm is alive and around us and is there to be encountered. Let's embrace the fact that the angelic realm isn't a realm to be afraid of, angels are in fact ministers sent from the Father on our behalf.

> *"Are not all angels ministering spirits sent to serve those who will inherit salvation?"*
>
> Hebrews 1:14

A DELIVERANCE PRAYER

I want to stop here for a moment and pray a simple prayer. If it fits, why don't you pray this out loud with me:

Father, I repent for believing that I could be deceived. For believing and fearing that I could be one of the deceived elect in the last days. I'm sorry for living in fear of the demonic realm. Forgive me for believing that greater is the demonic realm than the angelic realm. I thank you that there are more angels for me than there are demons against me. I thank you, Father, that You are for me and not against me. I thank You that You are a good Father and that when I ask You for good things, You don't give me a snake instead. I thank You that I won't receive a demon if I ask for Your Kingdom to come. I ask right now that any spirits of fear attached to the fear of being deceived go right now. I ask that Your Holy Spirit come and restore peace where I had the fear of being deceived. I also acknowledge that I have been seeing into the spirit realm. I repent for doubting that I was seeing angels. Forgive me for fearing that the shadows that I saw and the angels I felt around me, etc. were demons. I repent for that. I thank You that You are my protector and You have sent Your angels to be with me at all times. I thank You that I have constant protection and ministering angels around me at every given moment. I thank You that I am on the winning side and You are teaching me how to see the angels activated in my life. I trust You, Father God, with my life and every spiritual encounter I have I bring under subjection to Your name, in the name of Jesus I pray all this, Amen!!

Doesn't that feel good? A little spiritual detox is going on. We are getting free of fear. That is the first step to embracing the truth that you can see into the spirit realm. Now we can begin to embrace what God has always had for us. Now we don't have to fear. Now it's time to turn our fears into an intentional pursuit of the things of the Spirit and all that God has destined for us to enjoy.

Questions to Ponder

1. Have you had angelic encounters but did not recognize them as such? Why didn't you recognize them?

2. Do you see signs of the angelic? Lights, flashes, shadows, etc.? Describe.

3. Do you feel like fear could be holding you back from stepping into the supernatural realm at a higher level? How do you deal with that fear?

CHAPTER TWO

ENGAGING THE ANGELIC REALM

A ngels are for everyone to encounter and yet there is a wide spectrum of responses from people to the angelic realm. For some people, there seems to be a hands-off approach or even a flippant attitude towards angels. On the other hand, there are many people who get very wowed by others who encounter them because they believe only a special few can. And then some disconnect themselves entirely from the possibility of encountering angels. The truth is that every believer should expect to encounter, interact with, and partner with the angelic. After all, God sent them to minister to us.

Just so you don't think that angelic encounters are only for prophets, let's check out what the Scriptures say. In the book of Judges 13:2-9, we see that the life of Samson started with an angelic encounter to his parents, parents who were not prophets.

"A certain man of Zorah, named Manoah, from the clan of the Danites, had a wife who was sterile and remained childless. The angel of the LORD appeared to her and said, "You are sterile and childless, but you are going to conceive and have a son. Now see to it that you drink no wine or other fermented drink and that you do not eat anything unclean, because you will conceive and give birth to a son. No razor may be used on his head, because the boy is to be a Nazirite, set apart to God from birth, and he will begin the deliverance of Israel from the hands of the Philistines." Then the woman went to her husband and told him, "A man of God came to me. He looked like an angel of God, very awesome. I didn't ask him where he came from, and he didn't tell me his name. But he said to me, 'You will conceive and give birth to a son. Now then, drink no wine or other fermented drink and do not eat anything unclean, because the boy will be a Nazirite of God from birth until the day of his death.'" Then Manoah prayed to the LORD: "O Lord, I beg you, let the man of God you sent to us come again to teach us how to bring up the boy who is to be born." God heard Manoah, and the angel of God came again to the woman while she was out in the field, but her husband Manoah was not with her. The woman hurried to tell her husband, "He's here! The man who appeared to me the other day!"

AVERAGE PARENTS ENCOUNTER ANGELS

Samson's parents are just average parents. The mother of Samson encounters an angel who gives her specific instructions on how to raise Samson, who would become a deliverer for the oppressed people of Israel. She goes and tells her husband, Manoah. Manoah prays and asks God to send the angel back. God hears his prayer and sends the angel back to tell Manoah the exact thing that he had asked for.

Do you believe that you can interact with the angelic realm? Or do you believe that it's not meant for us? Manoah asked for another angelic encounter and he got it. He wasn't a prophet, he wasn't a preacher, he wasn't an especially "spiritual" person. He was simply a willing vessel, willing to be useful to the Lord. God entrusted him and his wife to raise Samson. There are so many things we can learn from this story, but the one thing that I am focusing on is to be like Manoah and ask! Don't be passive or lackadaisical with the supernatural realm. If you need something, ask for it. If you need an encounter with an angel, ask God to send one.

Angels are tangible. They are not impersonal, untouchable, or unapproachable. Angels have touched me and I have touched them. I have had many experiences where I would feel like someone poked me in the shoulder and when I looked around to see who was there, there was no one and nothing. While I no longer assume those experiences are all demonic, there are times when it has been. I have woken from a dream as I was being physically choked; that is demonic. The norm for the believer; however, is that we should expect to encounter heaven and the angelic realm. He is a relational God and wanted to have angels, creation, and animals, not just Himself and humanity. Creation is ours to bring heaven to, the animals are ours to rule, and the angels are ours to partner with.

You can read books about William Branham, the healing revivalist of the mid-1900's and how he had two healing angels. He wouldn't minister unless they were present. There was a photo captured of the angels around him. Many others have had accounts of capturing angels in a photograph or caught them on video or in audio form. A few years ago, Heather and I were ministering in a house in North Carolina. Pictures were taken during that time and later, when we looked at the pictures, we saw an angel right behind the person we were ministering to. My son, Micah, was the one who first saw the angel in the picture. Sometimes it takes the eyes of a child to see what is there. The angel in the picture looked a bit like I would imagine

Jesus to look, was as tall as the room and had colors coming out of certain parts of his body.

Consider the story of Moses and the burning bush in Exodus 3. Moses was working as a shepherd moving his flock around when he saw a bush that was burning but didn't burn up. Out of curiosity, he turned aside to go and see why and found himself in the middle of an encounter with the angel of the Lord.

> *"Now Moses was tending the flock of Jethro his father-in-law, the priest of Midian, and he led the flock to the far side of the desert and came to Horeb, the mountain of God. There the angel of the LORD appeared to him in flames of fire from within a bush. Moses saw that though the bush was on fire it did not burn up. So Moses thought, "I will go over and see this strange sight—why the bush does not burn up." When the LORD saw that he had gone over to look, God called to him from within the bush, "Moses! Moses!"*
>
> *Exodus 3:1-3*

ANGELS ARE PROFOUNDLY STRANGE AND WONDERFUL

How profoundly strange and wonderful all at the same time. That's how the angelic realm can be. Sometimes our brain tells us that if we were to have an encounter with God or the angels that it would have to be normal, like a human talking to a human. Moses had to encounter God with the angel of the Lord in a bush. He didn't see an angel, he saw a bush that talked! That is a funny picture if you think about it. Can you imagine the leader of a nation talking to a bush? That's exactly what Moses did. Notice in this passage that there is a reference to this encounter being with an angel, but also is God talking. It's a wonderful mystery that we see in certain scriptures in the Bible. How God and the angels were so closely aligned that at times you don't get a clear picture scripturally if it is God or an angel or both present in a situation. Sometimes it depends on the translation of the Bible you are reading. This causes us to walk in faith and trust that when we experience similar situations with the angelic and God, we don't have to be afraid of being deceived. We must trust that when we connect with an angel from the Lord, they are sent from heaven and heaven is trustworthy.

Part of the reason we don't experience the angelic more often is that we don't know how to engage the angelic. Moses had to 'turn aside' to encounter the angelic. I don't know how many times I have been in a room and an angel shows up but when I mention that an angel is there, people just continue with their conversations. They are similar to Elisha's servant who couldn't see what was right in front of him. In 2 Kings 6:17, it says,

"And Elisha prayed, 'Oh Lord, open his eyes so he may see.' Then the Lord opened the servant's eyes, and he looked and saw the hills full of horses and chariots of fire all around Elisha."

If you don't know what's there, you won't be able to access what it's there for. Ignorance can hurt you and in this situation, ignorance is not bliss. Ignorance will keep you from the encounters that could help you.

DISOBEDIENCE CAUSES YOU TO MISS OUT

Disobedience can also make you miss what's happening. Look at Balaam. He was a blind false prophet. Why was he blind? He was blind because he was not walking in obedience to God and did not have the right motives.

> *"Balaam got up in the morning, saddled his donkey and went with the princes of Moab. But God was very angry when he*

went, and the angel of the LORD stood in the road to oppose him. Balaam was riding on his donkey, and his two servants were with him. When the donkey saw the angel of the LORD standing in the road with a drawn sword in his hand, she turned off the road into a field. Balaam beat her to get her back on the road. Then the angel of the LORD stood in a narrow path between two vineyards, with walls on both sides. When the donkey saw the angel of the LORD, she pressed close to the wall, crushing Balaam's foot against it. So he beat her again. Then the angel of the LORD moved on ahead and stood in a narrow place where there was no room to turn, either to the right or to the left. When the donkey saw the angel of the LORD, she lay down under Balaam, and he was angry and beat her with his staff. Then the LORD opened the donkey's mouth, and she said to Balaam, "What have I done to you to make you beat me these three times?" Balaam answered the donkey, "You have made a fool of me! If I had a sword in my hand, I would kill you right now." The donkey said to Balaam, "Am I not your own donkey, which you have always ridden, to this day? Have I been in the habit of doing this to you?" "No," he said. Then the LORD opened Balaam's eyes, and he saw the angel of the LORD standing in the road with his sword drawn. So he bowed low and fell facedown."

Numbers 22:21-28

Balaam is written about in the book of Numbers. The word "numb" is in Numbers and Balaam was numb. That's a bit of a pun, but he was certainly walking in disobedience and because of that was not in tune with the angelic realm. How many of us are not in tune with the angelic realm because we are not walking in sensitivity, due to disobedience to the Spirit of God? Disobedience numbs the senses.

There are many things about the spirit realm that we need to be aware of and understand. There are things that we do without paying any attention to how it affects our own spiritual climate. Let me share an encounter I had with a spirit; the spirit of death.

PARTNERING WITH THE WRONG SPIRIT

A friend of mine, Rick, and I went to the mortuary to pray for a baby that had prematurely died. The family was devastated and they permitted us to go pray for the baby's resurrection. We were experiencing the presence of God during the prayer time but the baby did not come back to life. When I went home to my house that night a demon of death met me at my door. He looked like the typical grim reaper character you would see in a movie. I was immediately tormented by thoughts from that demon. The demon had followed me home from the funeral home. I cried out to the Lord and He told me something that profoundly changed how I behaved. He said, *"Keith, you love your death movies. You can't cast out what you are in agreement with."* You see the Lord had been after me for some time about the violent "guy" movies I enjoyed, typical blood and guts kind of movies. Now, I'm not releasing a law on everybody, I'm just saying what He was after in me. God then told me that in those movies I engaged with the spirit of revenge that wanted to see the bad guys killed. I couldn't partner with that spirit if I wanted to have authority over that same spirit when raising someone from the dead. It was a wake-up call for me to realize that things I did or allowed in the natural affected the spirit realm. We either get desensitized to the spirit realm and sometimes we can unintentionally invite the demonic realm to create a stronghold in our life.

I heard about a man whose son had continual encounters with angels and could see and engage with them. The man asked his son, "Would you ask the angels why I can't see them?" The angel replied, "It is because you have seen too much violence. If you will take some time to fast that violence out of your visual diet, then over time you too may start seeing the angelic."

I think there is validity to this sort of thing. It is not a law for everyone because we each have our own unique journey with the Lord. God can be after something in one of us and not after that same thing in another. The important thing is to be listening and paying attention to the Holy Spirit. I can watch a good guy movie now but there was a season where I did not have that same permission. Of course, I still guard my heart against partnering with a vengeful spirit but I've also found that I don't enjoy violent movies like I used to.

God always has something to say. There have been times in my life when He has wanted to speak something to me but I was too "busy". I love to watch good movies and during this particular season I kept sensing the Lord say, "*Why don't you turn the movies off early and come hang out with me in your bed?*" He would tell me to get my Bible and He would speak to me. Getting in bed early and reading my Bible seemed so boring and honestly, I didn't want to. But as soon as I yielded to Him, He started speaking to me. That season ended up being a profound time of revelation through the Word while I was simply resting in Him. Isn't it funny that the very thing that will bring life to us we often resist? God is so gracious that even when we fall short and are late in obeying He is still so merciful and gives us a second chance when we finally yield to Him.

Moses had to turn aside and Balaam had to repent from his disobedience (although Balaam didn't repent enough to save his life long-term). We have to learn to pay attention to the spiritual clues inviting us into a deeper connection with the spirit realm. If we want to walk with the Lord, and the angels He sends to help us, we have to understand how Heaven's protocol works. Heaven still and will always operate under the King's commands.

When we honor His commands we encounter Him and His helpers. When we dishonor His commands, eventually it will cost us.

HONORING THE KING IS ALWAYS BEST

Honoring the King and His values is the best way to make sure nothing is hindering us from experiencing Heaven's realm. If you have been walking in disobedience in an area that God has been speaking to you, it is time to turn away from that disobedience. Sometimes under the guise of not being 'under the law' anymore, people are actually totally bound up. I occasionally hear people saying things like, "Oh that's just legalism; you can do that under grace." To those that are naive like that, I remind them that Paul the Apostle says all things are lawful but not all things are profitable. So ask yourself if what you are doing is profiting you? There are certain things you can do that you can still go to heaven doing but you'll miss out on certain blessings here while on earth. For me, I don't want to miss out on any blessings, nor have any sin in my life; intentional or unintentional. As soon as Holy Spirit convicts my heart of an area where I am missing Heaven's mark I am going to do everything in my power, by the power of the Spirit, to take care of it. Why are we talking about this in an angel book? Because the angels honor Heaven's values and they partner in a greater measure with those who are in line with those values. Not everything about the spirit realm is clear but the key is to listen for Holy Spirit and above all else, guard your heart, for it is the wellspring of life. (Proverbs 4:23)

Maybe take a moment right now and ask Holy Spirit if there is something in your life that is hindering you from a fresh visitation from the Lord? Is there something He's been asking of you that you have been resisting or disobedient in? Is there something you are holding onto because you believe it's lawful, though not profitable, and it is preventing you from going to the next level?

If you answered yes, there is grace! Grace teaches us to be free of ungodly and worldly passions, it doesn't empower a license to looseness. Look at what Titus 2:11-12 says,

> *"For the grace of God that brings salvation has appeared to all men. It teaches us to say "No" to ungodliness and worldly passions, and to live self-controlled, upright and godly lives in this present age."*

Why am I belaboring this point? Because if you want to see and interact with the angelic realm, you have to honor the King of that realm. He wants to make known to us so much more than we could ever imagine. It is such a joy to begin to tap into some of those heavenly realities. Let us be a people that are set apart to Him. As you let go of the lesser you will be able to take hold of the greater. There are no regrets in having greater encounters with the King and His angels.

Questions to Ponder

1. Are you actively engaging the angelic realm or do you only wait for the supernatural realm to be God initiated?

2. What did you think of Keith's message that sometimes violent movies, or other influences like that, can hinder your authority with the demonic?

3. Is there anything that God is asking you to give up or even to do that could take you higher into fresh encounters with the Lord? Are you having a hard time obeying? If so, why?

CHAPTER THREE

TOUCHING THE ANGELIC REALM

The angelic realm is tangible, which means 'perceptible by touch'. I love to touch the presence of the angelic realm. I remember the first time I did that. I had just been reading in Genesis Chapter 32 about how Jacob wrestled with an angel of the Lord. Whether it was God or an angel is not crystal clear. Jacob wrestled with the angel until he received an upgrade in his identity. I was captured by the revelation that we could wrestle with the angelic realm and receive a blessing, and I have done that many times since then. The first time I wrestled with an angel was at a homegroup I was leading where the topic was angels. I was talking about wrestling an angel when one showed up. So I grabbed its ankle in the spirit and as everyone else was watching I was shaken around the room. It was a lot of fun. It reminds me of the story of Peter Pan wrestling with his own shadow.

Sometimes we think that angels are God's robots. We think that angels are not able to interact with us or us with them, but the opposite is true. Look at Samson's parents again and their encounter with the angel. They asked the angel to stay and he complied.

> *"The angel of the LORD replied, "Even though you detain me, I will not eat any of your food. But if you prepare a burnt offering, offer it to the LORD." (Manoah did not realize that it was the angel of the LORD.)"*
>
> Judges 13:16

That word detain also means 'hold back, refrain, withhold'. I believe we have the ability to affect and have a say in the spirit realm. I believe we can entertain angels and they enjoy hanging out because we keep their attention. Look at the three visitors who came to Abraham and told them of their plan to destroy Sodom. Abraham asked them to stay for a meal and they did. If you read the whole account and look closely, it seems that two were angels and one was the Lord, Himself.

> *"Let me get you something to eat, so you can be refreshed and then go on your way - now that you have come to your servant."*
> *"Very well," they answered, "do as you say."*
>
> Genesis 18:5

UNAWARE OF ENTERTAINING ANGELS

As you read throughout scripture, there are many angelic encounters where the person encountering them doesn't know they are encountering an angel. Manoah did not realize that he was entertaining the angel of the Lord until the angel disappeared through the fire into heaven.

> *"As the flame blazed up from the altar toward heaven, the angel of the LORD ascended in the flame. Seeing this, Manoah and his wife fell with their faces to the ground. When the angel of the LORD did not show himself again to Manoah and his wife, Manoah realized that it was the angel of the LORD."*
>
> Judges 13:20

There are wonderful mysteries for us to discover and it starts with knowing that we can have some impact in the angelic realm and can even host the angelic. There are times that we can literally partner with them, but often only after we've recognized they are there and then engage them.

SHAKING THE ANGELS HAND

Years ago I was on a platform preaching at a prophetic conference in Brazil. The conference was being led by a man who had been a part of the leadership of a large Baptist denomination. I saw that there were a few angels on the platform. Even for me, there are still times when I'm operating in faith with what I see happening around me. Sometimes you may know for certain you are seeing angels around and other times you may question if what you're seeing is real. I might see with my spiritual eyes an angel behind me, and other times I may see a flash or a shadow for a split second with my physical eyes. In this instance, I had a sense there was an angel next to me. That particular day I had been talking about the angelic and the supernatural realm. While I was speaking, I went over to grab the hand of one of the angels that were standing there. As I grabbed the angel's hand in the spirit, I was surprised to find myself thrown down to the ground, while attempting to hold on. Even more shocking was that, while there on the ground, the presence of God began to impact the place at a higher level. At one point,

I also saw three angels were standing in three portals. When I told people to go and stand where the angels and portals were, many got healed just by standing there. The Baptist leader was blown away and commented bewilderedly, "How is it that the Lord had to send this young minister to bring revival and help us show what revival is like?" He was baffled but blessed by the whole thing.

Sometimes believe the angelic realm and the physical realm are two totally different realms, and not related. We get wowed by the stories of those that have encountered heaven and think we'll only get to see heaven when we die. But what we need to realize is how tangible heaven is.

I love to grab God's hand and the angels' hands too. You might think that is a little far off, but it is biblical, as we've seen in the passage above. I like to encourage all of the prophetic students and emerging prophets that I train to make sure that what they're experiencing in the spirit realm is biblical, historically proven, as well as seen today as modern-day expressions of the Kingdom. Those are all important safeguards to have. What I am describing here may be far off your normal grid, but why not try and see what God reveals to you? What could it hurt?

Some time ago I found myself in the house of an influential person. I had known this person for several years and most of the time tried to be as normal as possible around him. Normal meaning that I hadn't let my 'ecstatic prophet side' out because I was trying to be on my best 'spiritual behavior'. Which is way overrated, by the way, I will admit. God is gracious when we are trying to look dignified with people, although there will be times when dignity will have to go if we want to move with Him.

Well, this particular day I had been having a nice chat with this man in his home. Nothing much was happening when all of a sudden a government angel showed up. How do I know it was a government angel? We'll talk more about that later. For now, I'll just say that I did what I always do when an angel shows up. I acknowledged the angel and then tried to touch it. As I went to grab its hand, all my calm and polite mannerisms were no longer possible to maintain as I went wild under the influence of the Holy Spirit. I started prophesying wildly over the man and then went jumping around the room releasing the joy of the Lord and prayers for his estate. It was quite a while later before I regained my calm demeanor again. You would think that this sort of thing would turn off an influential person but instead, it endeared him to me like never before. He began to dream with me on how he might partner with me to expand some of my prophetic ministry. It did the opposite of what I feared it would do. I thought it might turn him away from my ministry but it endeared him because the genuine me was coming out in a fuller expression. The negative atmosphere he had been under for a while lifted from him and his household. The fruit was evident. The way into that fruit was in partnership with the angel that God released. What a great and unusual encounter we had that day.

Now, there are times when touching an angel does nothing. Some angels are in the room simply as watchmen and are there to protect and watch over us. I can be around them and it will not release anything. I can even try to touch them and I won't be activated in my spirit with joy, or Holy Ghost electricity. When I see the angels that are more in the watchmen category in the room, I will still watch a TV show, relax, or enjoy my family. They're not always present to release a big encounter, but the main thing is that we *do* pay attention to them.

A CORRECT INTERPRETATION

Many times I've heard people say that we have to make sure we don't worship angels. Yes, I agree completely, but neither should we ignore angels. It'd be just like ignoring a person which would make them feel dishonored and devalued. There is a scripture that many use, out of context, that keep people from engaging with the angelic. It's in Colossians 2:18,

> *"Do not let anyone who delights in false humility and the worship of angels disqualify you for the prize. Such a person goes into great detail about what he has seen, and his unspiritual mind puffs him up with idle notions."*

People have built a huge doctrine around this verse, but the context is critical to its true meaning. This scripture wasn't written to tell us not to worship angels, it was written to tell the Colossians not to see an angel as a mediator between God and man. Back in those days, some believed that you couldn't get to God except through an angel. Paul was addressing that wrong belief. He was stating that Jesus was the way to the Father, not an angel. People who use this scripture to convince others to ignore angels are taking that scripture out of context. Of course, other scriptures tell us not to worship angels. The angels themselves tell us not to in Revelation 19:10,

> *"At this, I fell at his feet to worship him. But he said to me, "Do not do it! I am a fellow servant with you and with your brothers who hold to the testimony of Jesus. Worship God! For the testimony of Jesus is the spirit of prophecy."*

The true angels of God want nothing to do with being worshiped. If you have ever sensed or heard an angel trying to get you to worship them, you'd know immediately they weren't an angel of the Lord. Angels live to bring glory to God. We are not to worship angels but it is just as costly to ignore them.

Questions to Ponder

1. Have you ever touched an angel or been touched by an angel? Explain what happened.

2. Have you seen an angel show up that changed a situation into something positive? Share.

3. Have you ever stepped into a portal of glory? What happened?

CHAPTER FOUR

FINDING ANGELS

In the previous chapter, we talked about the powerful encounters that can happen when touching an angel's hand or body. Many times those encounters release something very intentional that God wants to do. Similarly, I have learned through my experiences that at times, for the assignment of the angel to be released, I have to be standing in the same location as the angel.

When I first began to grow in my confidence with what I was seeing, I would ask my prophetic friends, who also see in the spirit, to tell me of an angel's whereabouts. Sometimes I would see what they saw right away and other times I wouldn't. It didn't necessarily matter because I could still encounter the angels and receive what was being released.

One of my prophetic friends, while praying through our city with his family, had encountered and seen a particular angel that was connected to our city. My friend told me what part of the city and what street the angel was at. I felt it was important in that season to go look for that angel, so off I went. I didn't know the exact location of the angel but I had a general idea from the conversation with this prophetic friend. The area that I went to happened to overlook our city and when I finally discerned the exact spot, all of a sudden I started having an encounter. I was hearing things from Heaven about the keys to breakthrough for the city of Vacaville. It was powerful. It was that easy. I had to find the spot but when I did, the heavens were opened.

Some angels reside in certain locations. They may be there for a long time and they may be there for a few moments. The important thing is to understand why they are there and to partner with them when possible to see the assignment of Heaven fulfilled. There is a well-known story in the Bible with an angel at the pool of Bethesda. John 5:2-7,

> "Now there is in Jerusalem near the Sheep Gate a pool, which in Aramaic is called Bethesda and which is surrounded by five covered colonnades. Here a great number of disabled people used to lie—the blind, the lame, the paralyzed. One who was there had been an invalid for thirty-eight years. When Jesus saw him lying there and learned that he had been in this condition for a long time, he asked him, "Do you want to get well?"
> "Sir," the invalid replied, "I have no one to help me into the pool when the water is stirred. While I am trying to get in, someone else goes down ahead of me."

Whenever the angel stirred the waters people would get healed. People understood that being in proximity to that pool of water was important. They had to get into the water at the right time if they wanted to get well. Certain angels operate that way. They are positioned in a certain place for a certain time and a certain purpose. Once we get in alignment with the purpose, as well as get into the right location, a breakthrough happens.

GO TO WHERE THE ANGELS ARE

This is a fun key to the angelic realm. I love seeing the angels when I am preaching, or worshipping in my house, or simply going about my day. As I see them, most of the time I will go to where that spot is. Once I am in that spot I will try to calm my spirit down and pay attention to what I am seeing or feeling in the moment. Sometimes I ask out loud what is the purpose of the angel there. Joshua did the same thing.

> *"Now when Joshua was near Jericho, he looked up and saw a man standing in front of him with a drawn sword in his hand. Joshua went up to him and asked, "Are you for us or for our enemies?" "Neither," he replied, "but as commander of the army of the LORD I have now come." Then Joshua fell facedown to the ground in reverence, and asked him, "What message does my Lord have for his servant?"*
>
> Joshua 5:13-14

Some translations say, 'the angel of the Lord', others say, 'the Lord', and still others say, 'a man'. What's important here is the principle. Joshua approaches this awesome supernatural being and asks him a question. So can you. He asks the angel of the Lord if he is for or against them. Sometimes that is how it is in the spirit realm. People would like to think that there is no chance of being deceived if you are a true prophet or a real Christian but the truth of the matter is it's not always that simple. Joshua, who was often in the presence of the Lord, did not know whether the person standing in front of him was good or bad. Like I said before, there are certain tests we can use to determine whether an angel is good or bad. I have had angelic encounters only to find out later that they weren't good. How did I know? Firstly, the information released in the encounter wasn't fully biblical. That is how some people get off track. They may have an encounter that has biblical language. But if it does not align with scripture, it is not of God. That is where deceiving angels come into the picture. Even Satan himself used scripture out of context on Jesus. We read in Matthew 4:5-7,

> *"Then the devil took him to the holy city and had him stand on the highest point of the temple. "If you are the Son of God," he said, "throw yourself down. For it is written:" 'He will command his angels concerning you, and they will lift you up in their hands so that you will not strike your foot against a stone.'" Jesus answered him, "It is also written: 'Do not put the Lord your God to the test.'""*

DON'T JUDGE

We cannot assume that someone is a bad person because they had an encounter with an angel that wasn't from God because even Jesus did. Of course, we have to learn to discern between good and evil. One of the best ways to do that is to not operate in this realm alone. That is dangerous. The safest place to be in discerning the spirits is in a company of healthy prophetic people, kingdom leaders, and believers. Paul said a great way to tell if an angel was of God or not was if they preached the same Jesus he preached.

> *"But even if we or an angel from heaven should preach a gospel other than the one we preached to you, let him be eternally condemned!"*
>
> *Galatians 1:8*

Paul wouldn't have said an angel could preach a wrong gospel if it wasn't possible. I have had the wrong gospel preached to me and by God's grace, I was able to recognize it. When that happens you have to throw out the information you just received. That is why I talk to my mentors about what I am seeing in the Spirit, talk to my wife, and search out the scriptures as well as talk to the Lord.

I remember another time I had an encounter with an angel that was in my room and Heather said to me, "I don't know what spirit that is but it's not good." I was perplexed and honestly a bit irritated that she questioned me then. That is a red flag that you are not on the right track and the angel may not be right either. Never get defensive if someone asks you about an angelic encounter you've had. Always be willing to have your encounters processed by healthy, mature believers and leaders. We all need protection and in that place of safety, we don't have to live in fear because we trust that we are listening to the Holy Spirit and in good open and honest relationships with healthy people. When I say healthy people, I mean people that love the body of Christ, are connected to quality leaders who preach Jesus, walk in the power of God and love the presence of the Holy Spirit.

Why am I taking the time to share some of the false encounters I've had? It's to help you understand that it can happen to any of us. It happened to Jesus and it didn't make Him false. He was tempted and had an encounter with the devil in the desert. Testing your encounters does not mean something is wrong with you, it's wisdom.

On the other hand, I have witnessed believers having encounters in the spirit but as I listened to the language of what they were describing in their encounter I had to question their background. Others in the same room were having God encounters but, based on what the person described to me, it was clear that they had open doors from the past to the demonic. It causes a God encounter to have a mixture. When that happens, I'll ask them about their history and often find out that there were roots in the new age or some other false religion. At that point, I will walk them through deliverance from opening any spiritual doors up to those influences. Once those doors have been closed, they begin to have encounters that no longer have any mixture in them.

WHY IS THE ANGELS LOCATION IMPORTANT?

So why is it important to know, at times, the actual location of the angel? God can certainly meet us anywhere, but oftentimes He wants to meet with us somewhere specific. Have you ever had the Lord say to you to go to a certain place and when you went there, He encountered you? Abraham and Jacob both had that experience. They encountered the Lord at Bethel. Jacob encountered angels there. Elijah also knew that if he could get to the mountain of the Lord, he would encounter the Lord. It doesn't mean God can't speak to us anywhere but He's looking for faith and I believe that faith activates the encounter. Jacob's encounter at Bethel was so powerful that he set up a pillar as a reminder of the location where the heavens were opened and angels ascended and descended.

Once you've encountered God in a particular location it can become a place you revisit over and over for fresh encounters. I love going to the beach and for years that was always the place I knew that I would meet God. Sometimes I'd be going along doing life and then I'd realize how dry I felt. It was then that I would drive the forty-five minutes to the beach to spend a few hours encountering God in my special spot. I would sometimes come to the beach dry and bottled up in my spirit, and unable to hear. But by the end of the time spent there, I would have powerfully encountered God and left feeling energized and watered again. It wasn't that I was unable to hear the Lord at home and in my usual space. Sometimes you just need to get out of the bustle, anxiety, and busyness of what's familiar and get to a spot that you can relax, unwind, and hear God, if only for a few hours. It was always life-changing for me.

Sometimes it even has to do with expectation. Driving to the beach for me was an act of faith. I knew He would show up in fresh ways whenever I went there. Many churches are known as "revival spots" because they have hosted the presence of the Lord and seen the angelic realm break in through healing and miracles. Hungry people will go to those churches and will meet God. They go with expectation. Like I said before, it doesn't mean God won't meet with us anywhere, anytime. He longs to encounter us, even more than we do Him. But there is something powerful about our expectation and then action. There will be times when He is very specific in where He wants to meet us.

WHERE ARE THE ANGELS?

In the same way, the angelic can be that way. So start paying attention to what is going on around you. Where are the angels? Can you sense them? Do you know where they are and when they show up? Honor them when they are around. I am there to partner with them and to receive what the Lord wants to give me, in that location and moment. They are happy when I want to honor the Lord and I am happy too when the Lord shows up. It is an exciting adventure.

One day I was driving through a city where a friend was pastoring. I felt like I needed to stop by and say hi. So I did and we were enjoying a nice chat for a while. The conversation wasn't anything amazing and honestly, I was a bit tired. But then an angel showed up in the corner behind the pastor's desk. I casually got up from the couch I was sitting on walked over to stand where the angel was. As soon as I got into the exact spot where I saw the angel, I began to prophesy like crazy over the pastor. I went from tired and bored to rejuvenated and inspired. I prophesied things over the pastor that were very impactful for his present situation.

How many encounters have we missed out on because we have been nonchalant about the angels that are with us? It's time to let our expectations rise, our faith to move us to action, and to stop second-guessing ourselves. In the next chapter, I want to explore ways that will help us grow in our confidence about how we are seeing the angelic realm.

Questions to Ponder

1. Have you ever encountered an angel when you went to a specific location? What happened? Is the angel always in that same location or was it only one time?

2. Have you ever encountered a deceiving spirit? What did you learn from your experience?

3. What are three ways to safeguard yourself from being deceived in spiritual encounters?

CHAPTER FIVE

EVERYONE CAN SEE ANGELS

I hear people say all the time say that they wish they could see in the spirit, or I hear them say they don't see anything, period. I've spent years learning about the angelic realm and have come to the conclusion that everyone can see.

I remember a time some years ago when I was still discovering that I saw in the spirit realm. I had sensed two angels on either side of me, one on my right and one on my left. One of the prophetic guys in the room came and said to me, "Keith, I see two angels, one on your right and one on your left." What a great confirmation that was. There was another time when the same thing happened. I sensed two angels, one on either side of me and a young lady who saw in the spirit came up to me and said, "Keith, there are two angels behind you and they sure look fierce, they're warrior angels." It was another great confirmation and helped to build my faith that I was not alone.

SEEING THE ANGELS IS IMPORTANT

It's important to conclude for yourself that seeing angels and seeing in the spirit is necessary and a gift given by a good Father to His children. It's certainly true in the physical realm. One time I was running on a trail during one of my three-mile exercise routines. As I ran, I imagined running without any sight. I imagined stumbling over rocks in the road and roots from trees that had grown out of the ground. I imagined the hurt and damage that I would feel if I stumbled over them. I was thinking about not having eyes to see and comparing it to the blindness the Church has when it doesn't embrace the prophetic. The prophetic is the ability to see and hear what is going on in the spirit. The prophetic is seeing what God is doing, what the demonic is doing, and what is happening with humanity. The prophetic is also speaking to people's destinies and futures. I was feeling a passion build in me to fight for the Church to see again and to see the prophetic become a normal expression in our church.

STRANGE THINGS WE DO

Once in Brazil, there was a lady that was so desperate to see in the spirit. She was a pastor and asked me to pray for her spiritual eyes to be opened. Several times she had anointed her eyes and even done many prophetic acts over her eyes in hopes that her spiritual sight would be unlocked, but nothing had worked. I encouraged her that the first breakthrough for her was to believe that she was *already* seeing. Too many people don't believe they are seeing in the spirit because they are comparing themselves to others. They imagine that prophets or 'special ones' are those who see God, angels, and the spirit realm. When I first started growing in the prophetic the Lord gave me a verse. He gave me John 6:36, *"You have seen Me but you do not believe."* He started showing me that I believed if He showed Himself, it would be with lights, action, thunder, lightning, and flashes. It would have the 'wow factor'. He then took me through the scriptures and helped me see that the prophets were often seeing just like us; with the eyes of faith. Their seeing was also progressive. It wasn't this big, huge moment all the time where they were morphed out of their bodies, rather it was a step-by-step process of revelation.

In 1 Samuel 3, the Bible says, "*The word of the Lord was rare, there were not many visions.*" So the word of the Lord in that context was a vision. It wasn't a Bible verse like we have today all in one book. It was a mental picture that flashed across someone's mind. Sometimes we miss that God's voice is as simple as that, a vision, a mental picture flashing across our minds.

When God started training Jeremiah, He used the natural to speak to the spiritual. God asked him in Jeremiah 1:11, "*What do you see, Jeremiah?*" Jeremiah said, "*I see the branch of an almond tree.*" God told him, "*Good, you are seeing.*" Then He asked him again, what he was seeing. Jeremiah looked again and saw a pot tilting to the north. Then God gave him a prophetic word based on the tilting pot. God was using the physical realm to speak to Jeremiah; it was so simple. He was helping Jeremiah to see what was highlighted in the natural, what stuck out to him. This is a great way to tune into what God is saying. See what is highlighted to you in the natural and then ask God about it.

Have you ever been driving along a road and you see a couple of words up on a sign suddenly stick out to you? Or maybe you've been watching a movie with a lot of conversation and suddenly two short words stick out. These are invitations into seeing something in the spirit or hearing God's voice, but you have to lean into it. Follow those trains of thought if you want to discover what God is trying to say to you.

WHAT SEEING IN THE SPIRIT ISN'T

Seeing or hearing in the spirit doesn't necessarily mean you'll get full sentences, clear understanding, or a 'thus saith the Lord' kind of message. It can be that way, but most of the time we must partner with Holy Spirit in discovering what God is saying or doing. Daniel understood this key. We find in the book of Daniel, Chapter 7, that Daniel is lying on his bed and visions are flashing through his mind as he is resting. He writes down the substance of his visions and dreams. He is stewarding the information that he is getting. As you read further into the passage, he begins to have an encounter with the spiritual realm. He is not seeing something physical here, he is seeing something spiritual. He begins to see a throne with fire, the devil getting burned up, creatures, etc. There are times throughout the passage that you will notice that as he looks at something, the encounter goes a step further. He then begins to ask questions. He asks the angels questions, the Lord questions, and he thinks to himself about what he is seeing. This is the way that a prophet or prophetic people learn to hear and see in the spirit. They press into greater revelation, as they are hungry for more to unfold. Proverbs 25:2 says,

> "It is the glory of God to conceal a matter; to search out a matter is the glory of kings."

Growing in your ability to see the angelic realm and experience those types of encounters begins with believing. You *can* see in the spirit. You *can* hear what the Spirit is saying. Stop doubting; start believing. One of the roles of prophets is to help confirm to people that they are hearing from God. When some of my mentors helped to confirm what I was seeing in the spirit, that I was seeing angels, and that I wasn't blind, it furthered my journey to see at higher levels.

PRACTICING SEEING

As a practice, I often ask people if they see the angels when they show up in a room. I've spent years asking my wife and kids. They often will see exactly where the angel is. It took them a while to grow, just like it did for me. My son would beat himself up saying he didn't see anything but I would encourage him that he was seeing. There is always something going on in the spirit realm. We just need to pay attention. Sometimes it takes a prophet or a person who sees really clearly to remind us, but that is part of growing in this ability through community. I love that. If they ask you what is going on in the room or if you felt the angel walk in, that's an opportunity to turn on your spiritual sight and peer into the spirit realm. As you do, you will get more and more confident with what you see.

In this journey of growing, it is critical that we don't compare or disqualify ourselves because we're not seeing as someone else does. There are many ways to see. There are people that see, feel, hear, perceive, know, etc. We can feel things, hear things, see things in the natural, have visions, sense His presence, have a knowing in your 'knower' - all are valid. Ultimately, the goal is to connect to the spirit realm, not stay disconnected because we've disqualified how we see. I wonder what would happen if you just began to say out loud that you are seeing? Scripture says, 'let the blind man say I can see again'. That's a powerful declaration, especially in this context.

Sometimes I see angels show up in a room. Sometimes I will just sense a presence right next to me. Sometimes that presence is thick and other times it's less noticeable. Sometimes I will see the feet of an angel. Sometimes what I see is so vague and other times, with my spiritual eyes, I can see as clear as a bell. I don't often see the full angel with a face, hands, features, etc. Sometimes it's just an instant 'knowing'. Other times I see a sword being given to me, or a jar being poured out from an angel. It is often a momentary flash and then it is gone. But since I have been doing this for a while now, I don't discount what I am seeing. I know I am seeing something in the spirit.

CELEBRATE THAT YOU DO SEE

I try to encourage people to celebrate what they are seeing. I used to pray that I would see and encounter God more and more. I was never satisfied. I cried out, longing for encounters. I was partially crying out because I didn't feel like I was as good as Moses or Daniel or another great prophet because I hadn't had the kinds of encounters they had. I thought when I truly arrived I would be taken out of my body like Paul possibly was, or lifted up in the Spirit like John the Revelator. That is not the way to think. As God lovingly showed me, I realized that I was seeing in many of the same ways the prophets and prophetic people of the Bible saw. When we stop judging ourselves and begin celebrating what He is showing us, we will have more and more encounters.

I see so many who do the same thing. They invalidate what they're seeing. Or they're so insecure with their ability to see, they question everything. There are times when I can tell that they saw an angel but weren't confident enough to say so. That's when I will then tell them that I know they saw the angel. I saw their spiritual eyes look right at the angel, they just discounted it. After some practice, they will begin to see with more and more confidence. This is why we need mentors. Samuel needed a mentor, Eli, to help him start recognizing that what he was hearing and seeing in the spirit was God. Notice in 1 Samuel, Chapter 3:1,

> *"The boy Samuel ministered before the LORD under Eli. In those days the word of the LORD was rare; there were not many visions."*

Even though the passage starts with 'the word of the Lord was rare...in vision form', God started to talk to Samuel in the realm of hearing. He called Samuel's name. How is this connected to the fact that God was just talking about the rarity of visions? Maybe having visions and hearing God's voice are more connected than we think, and not separate categories. Notice God gave Samuel a message once Samuel finally responded to His voice. That leads me to believe that the voice Samuel was hearing, and the message that followed once he responded to the Lord, could fall under the "seeing" or "visions" categories.

WHY DO WE NEED TO CLARIFY HOW WE SEE?

Clarifying the ways we connect in the spirit realm is to bring greater definition and help launch us deeper into the things of the Spirit. Let's not categorize ourselves out of valid encounters we are having with God because we think we aren't seeing or hearing or don't have a gift like that person over there, or aren't having as "great" an experience as someone we have on a spiritual pedestal. Let's start enjoying what we are seeing and as we honor the little it will become much more. I stopped striving to see more in the spirit realm and I started resting in the fact that I was seeing. As I rested I began to see more. I also began to get around other prophetic people. One of the fastest ways to grow in the prophetic is to get around others that are prophetic. The same is true for seeing in the spirit. Get around others who see in the spirit. Remember, it is a gift from a good Father. God gave it freely, but we can grow in it as we hunger to know Him more. It is great to pursue gifts. I Corinthians 14 says to earnestly pursue the gifts, especially prophecy. I would put seeing in the spirit and the many ways we see, under the realm of prophecy or the revelatory gifts; which includes other gifts like words of knowledge, discernment of spirits, and prophecy.

EVERYONE CAN SEE, I REPEAT, EVERYONE!!

Everyone can see. Everyone sees in different ways. The main point is that we recognize it as a gift, celebrate what we see, celebrate what others see, and stay in a place that is provoked for more of God. God gave the prophetic, the prophets, the angelic for our benefit to help build up the body of Christ. Seeing the angelic realm shows us what God wants to do *now*.

Just like Elisha prayed for his servant Gehazi to see in the spirit, I pray that your eyes would be open to perceive and see what God is doing in a greater measure and to understand more fully how you see. I pray that you would stop disqualifying yourself in any way. Seeing is the natural order for those who are sons and daughters of God.

Questions to Ponder

1. According to this chapter, what are some ways you could be hearing from God?

2. Why do you think you second-guess what you are hearing or seeing?

3. Do you have anybody who you can process seeing the angelic with?

CHAPTER SIX

WHAT'S YOUR NAME MR. ANGEL?

Learning to partner with angels is exciting, important, and necessary. We can't partner with God's helpers if we don't know they are around us. Neither can we partner with them if we doubt that we can see in the spirit or if we disqualify ourselves because we deem others more spiritually in tune than us. Once we have settled these issues, it's time to move into the next level of partnership with the angelic.

A few years back I was in South Africa and a friend of mine told me something that seemed strange and frankly questionable to me. He said, "Keith, I talk to the angels and I ask them their names." It is interesting that in some areas of our life we can feel so spiritually advanced but in other areas, we are limited because of a belief that certain spiritual principles are 'off limits' for a believer. This hit my "off-limits to a believer" button. I've had many of those buttons pushed over the years. I used to think joy in the church was unacceptable, now I know it is vital for a victorious Kingdom believer to carry joy. Asking an angel their name was definitely stretching me. I'm not trying to build a doctrine around asking an angel their name, but I do believe that if we find biblical precedence for something, then we have permission to step into the same thing knowing that it can help us advance the Kingdom.

When my friend told me he asked his angels what their names were I was hesitant. Maybe I had a fear of being outside the bounds of good safe Christian practices but maybe I also had a bit of doubt that I could hear an angel tell me their name. I was about to have my faith stretched.

AN ANGEL NAMED PETER

A couple of days after that encounter, I was sitting in the office of a pastor waiting to preach in his church in South Africa. As I was sitting there, I saw an angel appear in the middle of the room. I decided to take a chance and ask the angel's name. I didn't know if I would hear or discern anything. I have learned since then that how I hear the name can come in a variety of ways. Surprisingly, I sensed in my spirit that the angel's name was Peter. Now that's biblical and safe, right? As I heard that name, I began to get a message that night for the church I was going to speak at for the first time. The name Peter launched me into a message about the life of Peter. I went out that night to preach armed with a word about Peter. After the worship, the meeting was turned over to me. Since I had never been there before I only knew the name of the pastor. As soon as I got up, I called the worship leader out and began to prophesy over him. After I gave the word, I asked him what his name was. He said his name was Peter. I was pleasantly surprised. Could I be onto something? Could this 'asking the angel's name' thing be something? Then I called out another random person in the church and began to prophesy over him as well. When finished I again asked him his name. His name was also Peter! It was then that confidence grew in me. I was tapping into something. This name thing was valid. I knew with certainty that the message given to me about the life of Peter was from the Lord and gave the word boldly to the congregation that night.

As I began to grow in this new discovery, I found a variety of different keys. Let me share one. I believe the name of the angel can sometimes be about the assignment of the person I am to connect to. Once when I was back in my hometown of Vacaville, California I sensed an angel was in the room one morning. I asked the angel its name and sensed its name was Tom. Later that same day I went to a coffee shop and met someone unexpectedly whose name was, you guessed it, Tom. I knew instantly that I had something for him. I was beginning to realize that when I get an angel's name, I am sometimes getting the name of my assignment for that day.

Look at the story of Peter the Apostle when he was locked up in prison and an angel freed him. Peter went and knocked on the door of John and when the servant answered the door, he closed it and went back to the people in the house reporting that an angel of Peter showed up. I have discovered that sometimes the name of an angel is also the name of the person that the angel has been assigned to and they are there to help us deliver a message to that particular person. I've seen that happen over and over again in my life.

WHAT SHOULD YOU BE ASKING THE ANGEL?

Sometimes the angel doesn't answer the question we *are* asking but the question we *should* be asking. When I ask them their name they tell me their assignment. For instance, once I asked an angel their name and they answered, "serenity". That angel's name was their role as well; to bring peace.

I appreciate that. Sometimes their name isn't important to know; but often when you do know their name, you know why they're there.

One day I asked my son Micah about his angel's name and he told me his name was Michael. Michael stays in his bedroom. I believe some people have angels assigned to them for a season or a lifetime according to their needs and assignment of that season. Sometimes an angel is only there for a day or two, or even a few minutes. Sometimes an angel is there as a watchman and you won't hear much at all from them when at other times you will get a lot of traction around them. When they are a watchman angel, they are there to guard and protect so you may not have a lot of interaction or revelation from them because that is not their purpose.

ANYONE SEE 333?

I remember a season where I was always seeing the numbers "333". I asked the Lord about it and He told me Jeremiah 33:3, *"Call to Me and I will show you great and mighty things you know not of."* Every time I saw that number I would start to pray to understand the mysteries God wanted to show me. Then, at times, I would have an angel show up. I began to realize that this angel was there to help me discover the mysteries that I had been praying to know. I found myself having sudden revelations concerning a variety of things that I could never have understood on my own. It was and still is an exciting time when this angel of revelation shows up.

It started to become clear that this angel surrounding my revelation of Jeremiah 33:3, might also be found in scripture, or at least the same kind of angel. As I searched deeper, I found that Samson's parents also had an encounter with a similar angel. They did the very thing I initially thought was so stretching, they asked the angel for his name. The angel answered Samson's parents, "Why do you ask me my name? My name is 'Beyond

Understanding.'" It could be that the angel meant they wouldn't have been able to understand his name, but in this season for me, I was convinced there was an actual angel named, "Beyond Understanding". And this angel's role was to help me tap into the '33:3 of God', to understand the things that only God can reveal, the mysteries, the great and mighty things that I did not know. So now, anytime this angel shows up, I get revelation that I wouldn't know otherwise. (Is it a coincidence that when I went to edit this part of the chapter my computer was at 33% power at 1:33? There's that 33 again… I just love the way God talks.)

UNDERSTANDING WHY

We must understand why the angels are there. Sometimes their name reveals the 'why'. Discovering their names can be so helpful in finding out what God wants to do or give to us for a particular assignment or season. Next time you sense or see an angel in the room, turn in the direction of the angel and ask them their name. Calm your spirit down to hear and press into the encounter. Sometimes you may not hear anything, but other times it will ring in your ear loud and clear. I usually try to get right where the angel is, then try to shake their hand, engage my spirit to worship God, or even say hello to the angel. If I don't sense anything particularly significant happening as I am pressing into this encounter, then I continue with my day. It's not necessary to make something happen, angels just like to hang around us. Sometimes their assignment isn't clear and isn't necessary for me to engage with. The point is to let it be an adventure with God. It is one that I am continually on, and the journey of learning is filled with wonder and joy.

Questions to Ponder

1. Have you ever asked an angel their name? What did they say? Did it speak to you about the angel's assignment?

2. Did it feel like a stretch to you to ask an angel their name? Have you been able to settle your fears through the scriptures in the Bible that talk about asking an angel their name?

3. When you realize that an angel is sent from God, how do you fully engage with the angel to receive what God sent them to give you?

CHAPTER SEVEN

DIFFERENT KINDS OF ANGELS

If angels are sent to minister to the heirs of salvation then we must pay attention to what they are ministering. Sometimes it is very evident as seen in the introduction of this book when I shared the first time Heather and I were ministered to by an angel. We were refreshed by the end of the encounter and our love came back even for those who were against what we were bringing. There are many different purposes and types of angels who bring joy, hope, peace, love, vision, strategy, among other things.

One of the angels that I love to have around is similar to the angel I called 'Beyond Understanding'. Let me share a story about that angel. One day I was suddenly aware that a spirit or angel of revelation was present. Paul talks about this in Ephesians 1:17, when he was praying for the spirit of revelation,

> *"I keep asking that the God of our Lord Jesus Christ, the glorious Father, may give you the Spirit of wisdom and revelation, so that you may know Him better."*

I think that 'spirit' could be two things. It could be the Spirit of God bringing revelation and/or it could be God bringing revelation through an angel. That day it just seemed like an endless stream of revelation flowed to me concerning a theology shift that I needed. God upgraded my view of the Word through a several hour encounter with this angel. During this encounter, I found that it didn't matter if I left to eat or do other things because when I came back to my prayer room, the angel was there ready to open up fresh revelation to me again and again. That is an exciting purpose for an angel to be sent to us for. When God starts breathing on His Word, or starts taking us through an encounter that gives us a message to speak, a Kingdom value to gain understanding on, or simply a word to encourage us, we need to pay attention to the angel of revelation that is present and posture our hearts to take time to receive what they are bringing.

MISSING THE ANGELIC VISITATION

I remember hearing several prophets confess that God came or sent an angel to them with a little rebuke saying, *"I wanted to come to you for the last months but you were too busy and missed what I have wanted to bring."* How many times have we missed the angelic because we were busy, distracted, or disobedient? Like Balaam, we can have an angel standing right in front of us wanting to chat with us but we are so locked into motives that are not of the kingdom that we are missing out on the message God wants to bring us. Numbers 22:31-34 says,

> *"Then the LORD opened Balaam's eyes, and he saw the angel*

> *of the LORD standing in the road with his sword drawn. So he bowed low and fell facedown. The angel of the LORD asked him, "Why have you beaten your donkey these three times? I have come here to oppose you because your path is a reckless one before me. The donkey saw me and turned away from me these three times. If she had not turned away, I would certainly have killed you by now, but I would have spared her." Balaam said to the angel of the LORD, "I have sinned. I did not realize you were standing in the road to oppose me. Now if you are displeased, I will go back."*

Thankfully God is gracious and meets us in those times even though we may be late in receiving what He tried to bring earlier. Hopefully, we learn our lesson and posture our hearts and lives in such a way that we don't miss the next encounter He brings our way.

THE ANGEL OF AWAKENING

Another angel I love to encounter is the angel of awakening. A while back I was ministering prophetically to a prophet and I saw that he was being highly impacted by my words. He said he had been praying for a year about what he was now hearing in the prophetic word I was releasing. He then asked me to come up to his hotel room where he and his assistant were hanging out. After a few minutes of chatting in his room, a huge angel showed up. I was only able to see his legs, as the angel's body went up through the roof of the hotel. Doing what I often do, I reached over to get my hand near the vicinity of the angel. As I said before, sometimes proximity activates the encounter for me. As soon as I touched the angel I began to prophesy like crazy. For what seemed like an hour I continued to prophesy about the move of God that was coming to California. Locations of different hot spots were revealed and much more came from this encounter. The other prophet was getting texts from the host of the evening meeting asking where he was. He kept thinking he needed to stop the encounter and get to the meeting. The Lord told him clearly that if he looked at his watch again he would miss what God wanted to do. The encounter was so powerful that we were both taken back by what the Lord gave us during that time. Since then I have had that same angel present in different meetings where I am at or in places I know God wants to move mightily. The angel of awakening is there to stir up people's passion for the presence of God. Song of Solomon 2:7 says,

> *"Daughters of Jerusalem, I charge you by the gazelles and by the does of the field: Do not arouse or awaken love until it so desires.."*

There is an awakening of intense love that God desires but we have to be ready for it. God is looking to bring a move of His Spirit and releases angels to help facilitate that. In Zachariah 4:1 we see an angel awakening Zechariah, *"Then the angel who talked with me returned and wakened me, as a man is wakened from his sleep."*

This is another place where we see an angel of awakening at work. There are so many clues in the Scripture, for those with eyes to see and hunger to understand. The Lord is after His bride's heart and when the angel of awakening is sent, it is there to stir up love in the hearts of the people for their King. 'Do not awaken love until you're ready'. In other words, when this invitation is extended, you have to be ready to give *all*. His love is all-consuming. I love to respond to the angel of awakening because He is sent from the Father to restore our first love, to get us out of a lukewarm state. If we don't respond when we begin to feel the stirrings, we will miss the day of our visitation. The Lord told me once that He was pursuing us. He longs for us more than we can imagine and He sends His angels of awakening to stir us up in love for Him because He's so ready to engage with us intimately.

ANGELS THAT INSPIRE PROPHECY

Another angel I have experienced is an angel of prophecy. As I mentioned in another chapter, there were angels who ministered with William Branham as he moved in powerful words of knowledge and miracles of healing. I have also experienced this kind of angel that brings prophecy. There are times when I don't feel like prophesying but as soon as I step into the vicinity of an angel that releases prophecy, I am immediately hit with the spirit, unction, and passion to prophesy. There are times when I have prophesied over many people by stirring up the prophetic gift from within. Other times I may have a very specific assignment from the Lord to prophesy over someone in particular, and once that is over, I am done with prophesying. Each of these experiences is valid. There is also the joy of partnering with an angel to release the prophetic.

Recently I was at an event where a number of leaders were present. There was one particular person I wanted to prophesy over and so I found the opportunity to release what God was saying over them. Then there was another person next to them that I also felt led to prophesy over. But after that, I felt done. Of course, when people see me prophesying at a high level with power and authority often they will want to pull on that anointing for themselves too. But the strange thing is that when the angel is no longer present, I no longer have a passion to prophesy. I had several people waiting for me to pray over them after that but had to tell them that the angel had left and because of that, I was finished prophesying. I assured them that if God had a word for them, He would bring the angel back. It is a bit humorous at times but it also freeing for me as well.

It reminds me of the encounter that Saul had with the company of prophets. Saul got into the presence of the prophetic company and began to prophesy rapidly and fully to the point that the people were perplexed and said that Saul is now also counted among the prophets. They knew that this was unusual. There are wonderful mysteries we find in Scripture. The main thing is that we get to learn to partner with the Lord and discover at times that certain angels are released on our behalf with specific targets.

Another type of angel that I've encountered are angels over cities. I love going into a city to find out what the particular angel, city, and church-type that city is. I often ask God to show me what type it is, according to the Book of Revelation. If you read Chapters 2 and 3 in the Book of Revelation, you will find that seven angels were given assignments and messages for seven churches in different cities. I believe every city today can be likened to one of these seven cities spoken of in Revelation. For instance, I pastored in the city of Willits. After studying for a while on this subject it became obvious to me that Willits was a 'Philadelphia City'. This particular city has an angel assigned to help steward the key of David. What I learned about this type of city was that if you wanted to be successful and see breakthrough, you had to learn to war with worship. You had to know your authority. You had to be willing to persevere even if you were small in number. I believe these city angels are positioned to help churches bring a specific and targeted breakthrough for that region. If you are trying to follow the blueprints of an 'Ephesus City', but you are in a 'Philadelphia City', you won't see the desired breakthrough. Align yourself with the purpose of God that has been given to that particular city angel and you will find greater breakthrough.

I know that the angels over cities get excited when we are lined up to what that city's purpose is. When I moved to Vacaville, I heard the Lord say that the city was Laodicea. Now, of course, I wasn't too happy about that because Laodicea had always gotten a bad rap. It was the city known to be lukewarm. But then I heard the Lord say that the redemptive purpose of our city was to be a place that is on fire for God.

YOUR CHURCH HAS A SPECIAL ANGEL

There are also angels of churches. Many times when I go into a church, I will see several large angels hanging around. After I get acquainted with them, I start to get strategy for that church, for their city, region, etc. Then when I begin to preach, pray, or minister I will release that strategy to the people which awakens them and the leaders to get excited because many times I am tapping into something that they have already been pressing into and God wants to reveal their next steps for breakthrough. There is now a resonance that begins to happen in the spirit between the angels, the people, the leaders, and the Lord. God is always looking for people on earth who will partner with the angels that are assigned to certain locations and churches. Once the saints, the leadership, and the people get synced up with the assignment of the angels that God has released then breakthrough comes. Praise the Lord for this. That is why I would encourage you wherever you are, whatever church you're in, city you're apart of, or area you live in to begin to ask the Lord about the angels assigned there. Ask Him to show you where they are. Get some other intercessors together and prophetic people and pray and see what God will have you to do to partner with the angels to see greater breakthrough.

There are many types of angels for many types of reasons. I have just mentioned a few different types to whet your appetite for what is available to partner with. Let's make it a point to discover what purposes God has assigned to the angels He sends us and begin to move with them to see greater breakthrough and more synergy than ever before.

Questions to Ponder

1. Have you encountered any of the angel types Keith talked about in this chapter? Share what your encounter was like.

2. Have you ever been rebuked by the Lord for being too busy and missing out on an angelic encounter? What did you learn from that rebuke? How can you better position yourself to not miss the next encounter?

3. What kind of city do you think your home city is in connection with the seven cities in Revelation? What clues does that reveal about how to get a greater breakthrough in your city?

CHAPTER EIGHT

PARTNERING WITH THE ANGELIC

It is clear throughout Scripture that angels are sent to minister to us, bring messages, provide protection, and breakthrough. Our partnership and agreement with them are vital. Have you noticed how there are majors and minors in Scripture? For instance, there is a major emphasis on prophecy being for the purpose of encouragement, exhortation, and comfort. But there is a minor emphasis on how, as people can prophesy through prayer, the gift of tongues, with words of knowledge, etc. Certain things are preference and certain things have a higher priority biblically. It is same with the angelic realm. We should major on the fact that God says angels are sent to minister to us, but minor on the many ways people can see and partner with them.

LEARN THE ANGELS COLOR

One of the ways that I began to partner with the angelic was knowing the color of the angel. This has become a big source of encouragement and confirmation for me in the variety of ways God asks me to minister. One day I was getting ready to speak at a meeting and one of my intercessors told me that they saw a red angel there. I immediately knew that it was time to stir the saints up into a place of passion for the Lord, where God was going to move in a revival spirit opening people's hearts up with a hunger for more of Him. I was already leaning in that direction as I had been praying before the meeting for what God wanted to do. But when I heard from my intercessor that a red angel was there, I was fully convinced. Sometimes I have the luxury of getting a word from the Lord in advance but often I hear nothing until I am getting ready to speak. In this case, once I knew that a red angel was there, I could confidently partner with that angel to stir up passion and bring breakthrough to the meeting.

Other times I've had an intercessor, who may be thousands of miles away, see a blue angel in the room. When that happens, I know that God wants to release revelation and, most of the time, have already been preparing to release a word of revelation for that region or church. When I hear that a blue angel is there I now have the extra confidence to know that I need to deliver the word the Lord has given me. Now could I deliver the word without the angelic help? Yes, I could, but it is very helpful to have that confirmed, and at times I am in an internal battle on what I should do. This is a battleground and the victory may be won or lost based on the intel the intercessors send me. This is similar to a real physical battle in a war. If there is no communication between the commanders leading the army and the soldiers then victory will not be possible. Communication helps the soldiers in the battle see the greater battle plans. That is what partnering with the angelic is like. We are tapped into angelic agents that are there to help the Commander and Chief, God Almighty, bring victorious strategies to our situations. The angels are there to help and the intercessors are paying attention to what God wants to do. This is a great Kingdom partnership between the intercessors, the angels, and me that benefits me and those that I am ministering to. Having prophets and prophetic intercessors in your life are a great source of encouragement and often confirm what God is already saying or doing. They can also give insights into something that I wasn't seeing at all. I am thankful for both forms of intercessory help.

I love being able to catch the clues that help me know what the angels are there for and in doing that I now know what the Lord is up to. The angels are a part of the Lord's strategic army and so many times an answer to our prayers comes in the form of an angel as they are released on our behalf. Daniel understood this as we see in Daniel Chapter 9 and 10. It says that as soon as he began to pray an angel was released on his behalf in answer to his prayer. Angels are dispatched as a part of God's answers to our prayers. What if He sent angels but we weren't paying attention? What if the answers to our prayers were in limbo because we didn't believe in the angelic? Acts 10:3-6 shows us the importance of the angelic in the role of a harvest that touched a new people group. Cornelius's prayers and generosity released the angel to visit him and the Spirit to visit Peter to open up Cornelius's entire household to salvation,

> *"One day at about three in the afternoon he had a vision. He distinctly saw an angel of God, who came to him and said, "Cornelius!" Cornelius stared at him in fear. "What is it, Lord?" he asked. The angel answered, "Your prayers and gifts to the poor have come up as a memorial offering before God. Now send men to Joppa to bring back a man named Simon who is called Peter. He is staying with Simon the tanner, whose house is by the sea."*

This was a big deal because it was outside of the normal grid for that time for Jews to minister to the Gentiles. It took the angelic, Spirit encounters, and trances to get that accomplished. Learning the different ways that God answers prayers and how we can partner with God is key to continued breakthrough. What if some of the lack of breakthrough we've experienced is our inability to effectively recognize and partner with the angels God has sent on our behalf?

THE ANGEL OF BREAKTHROUGH HAS CONDITIONS

Sometimes God releases the angels with a breakthrough that is dependent on our specific obedience to what the Spirit reveals for us to do. For example, I was preaching in South Africa once when the Lord started giving me a whole message for the body of believers that night about the need for one-on-one ministry. There are times to minister to the whole and there are times to minister to the one. At that moment, God was emphasizing the importance of ministering to the one person that He puts in their path. As I began to release my message, I saw a large angel show up with a very small dagger in his hand. Many times I just see a vague outline of an angel when one shows up, but this time I saw something specific. When I looked at the dagger I saw that it had jewels on its handle. It was very clear. I was seeing this while I was speaking. This was one of those moments when many things are happening all at once. I was speaking to the people, seeing the angel, and thinking about what it meant to have the dagger while also wondering what God was doing in the meeting. All of a sudden I realized that the reason I hadn't gotten breakthrough yet that night was that I was also supposed to minister one-on-one to people during that meeting. Then the message He gave me would get traction. The angel with the dagger was showing me that a dagger is for close combat. If I were to get the victory that night I would have to step out in faith and minister to an individual in a very personal way to unlock the victory.

Interestingly, there are moments where it takes faith to minister to the one when you are more comfortable with the crowd and at other times it's more comfortable ministering to the one than the crowd. This was the former. I felt nervous about ministering to one person. What if the ministry didn't affect the whole crowd? I do a lot of public prophecies where I call someone out and prophesy over him or her but this was different for some reason. I decided to step out in faith. I saw a man in the audience that was highlighted to me and began to minister to him. I took my time making sure he got ministered to with the heart of the Lord. Heidi Baker models this so well. She will take time for the one in a crowd of thousands while she is the main speaker. It demonstrates the heart of the Lord for the one.

This was one of those moments. The beautiful thing was, as I ministered to the one the Lord would highlight another. They would get touched and then He would show me another, and then they were highly impacted. The impact caught the whole room on fire and by the end of the night, it was clear that breakthrough came as I partnered with the specific assignment God had sent the angel to release. What a great pleasure to partner with the Lord and His angels in this way.

LEARNING THE SPECIFICS OF SPIRIT LANGUAGE

God loves variety and there are many ways He chooses to minister to us and through us. Learning how to listen to the specifics of the Spirit is key to *effective* ministry. I know that oftentimes the spirit realm operates when we get in sync with that realm. If God sends an angel of hope and we are trying to speak on faith, we are out of sync and won't see the same level of breakthrough that's possible. There are Kingdom principles that we can use anytime like tools in our toolbelt. I can speak in tongues anytime I need encouragement. I can worship when it is the time in the service to worship. I can pray for the sick when a sick person is present and asks me to pray for them. But then there are times when God has very specific plans about how He wants to do things. It is in *those* times that we can't rely on the general principles of the Kingdom. We have to be led by the Spirit and do what He says. But when we don't feel anything specific from the Lord, we simply step out by faith and activate whatever spiritual principle we feel we should use for that time.

If God releases an angel on our behalf that is carrying joy but I want to go into deep intercession with tears then I will miss what God is doing. The joy is there and is for my benefit but I have chosen to go into the room of deep intercession. It is a room that I can always go into because God has given me access to that Kingdom principle but it is not always timely to do so. That is why Jesus told His disciples in Matthew 7 that there would be those who prophesied in His name but did not know Him. The word 'know' in this passage is "ginosko" which is where we get the word 'intimacy' between a husband and wife. Let's not be the ones who operate solely on principles and miss out on the intimacy of knowing Him fully.

Early on in my journey, I had one of my prophet mentors tell me that if a preacher was ministering on healing in a meeting, had just finished preaching about it, and was now laying hands on people for healing that I needed to partner with what God was specifically doing in that meeting. I could minister in joy and prophecy for an individual during that time if I wanted to, but if I ministered healing I would see a greater breakthrough.

There have also been times when I have preached on healthy relationships or something of that nature. When the meeting was over, a number of folks came up for personal prayer, many of whom wanted prayer for healing in their body. But at that moment, I knew that God was dealing specifically with relationships. One person had a hip issue and I told them that their healing was connected to relational health. They may have needed to break soul ties with someone and once they did, their hip would be healed. The healing for that night was mostly connected to the relational anointing that God was pouring out.

It is best to emphasize what the Lord is going after so you can see a greater partnership with heaven and the breakthroughs that come as a result. Once again, I am reminded of Balaam who was going somewhere that God did not want to go. He was trying to come into partnership with someone that God did not want to partner with. The angel was on the road to resist him and kill him if necessary. Angels can change course for minor things but they are not prone to disobedience like we are, and must stick to their main assignment. The angels ascend and descend which often means they ascend back to heaven when their assignment has been accomplished and they descend back down to earth with fresh assignments.

KNOWING YOUR SEASON HELPS

Another key to partnering with the angelic is to understand what season the Father has us in. Knowing what He is doing in our current season will help us discern how to better partner with Him and His angels assigned to us for that season. Sometimes He wants us in a season of rest but we are working so hard. Other times He has us in a season of plowing but we are trying to rest. We have to understand what He is doing to partner most effectively with Him. The sons of Issachar understood the times and seasons and we too should be a prophetic people who understand the times and seasons. What season am I in? What is God presently doing? What is He going to do? What has He already done? What is for now and what is for later?

One simple way to discern what season you are in is to ask the Lord what He wants to be for you in this season. Or tune into what He's been declaring to you about who you are. Sometimes you can also look at what the enemy has been trying to disrupt as well, and that will clue you into what season you're in. These three things help me most effectively know what season I am in and also help me hone in on how to partner with the angelic in that season.

We know that the angels are here for God and serve His purposes, and they also serve those who are God's. When we partner with Him and His angels, we will achieve acceleration and breakthrough.

Questions to Ponder

1. Have you seen an angel who was a particular color? What did the angel's color reveal to you about their assignment?

2. What season are you in? Rest, work, battle? Are you out of alignment with your season and perhaps the angels that God has sent?

3. What can you do to become better aligned?

4. Can you tell what the enemy is up to in this season? What does the enemy's strategy tell you about what God is doing and what He has sent His angels for?

5. Take time to agree and align with God's season for you.

CHAPTER NINE

ANGELIC ACTIVITY

In the first chapter of the Book of Hebrews, we are told that angels are sent to minister to 'those who will inherit salvation'. This gives us a reference point that basically tells us they can minister to *a lot* of people. One of the things I have learned over the years is that, while they can minister to many, they seem to hang out with certain people; those who are doing the Father's will, not ashamed of Him, and advancing His Kingdom.

I remember one of the first times I saw the Father cheering over me in heaven with angels present. I had been doing a joy-walk through seven cities throughout Humboldt County and Mendocino County. I share this story in several of my other books. That first day was especially rough as I was dancing along the main 101 highway with a jester's hat on. I was with other intercessors who were also praying with me through those seven cities. I knew the act of wearing the hat and dancing foolishly before the

King of Kings; showing I was His fool and no one else's, would continue to break the stronghold of fear in my life. As the day began, I felt the fear and even some resistance from the intercessors. My faith was being stretched. Then I saw the heavens open and the Father standing there cheering me on saying, "That's my boy! I'm so proud of you, son!" There was a sense that the angels were present witnessing this whole event unfold. I have learned that angels like to hang around those who are not ashamed of God. Luke 12:8-9 says,

> *"I tell you, whoever acknowledges Me before men, the Son of Man will also acknowledge him before the angels of God. But he who disowns Me before men will be disowned before the angels of God."*

I think 'acknowledging Me before men' can mean a variety of things in a variety of seasons. For me, at that moment, it literally meant dancing for the Lord in front of people which, established in my life. that He was the One Who's praises I lived for, not for man's. The angels see those acts and see who the Father is pleased with and they like to partner with them. They want to be around those who live for the Father. Now, because the Father is so good, angels are even with people who resist Him because that's their assignment. But I believe that angels absolutely love the presence of God, just like many of us do. They love the worshiping heart that cultivates the presence of God and when I am in the presence of God they too get to enjoy what I am enjoying. When I am resisting the presence of God they are aware of that as well.

ANGELS AREN'T STUCK EMOTIONALLY

Some may think that angels are stuck in some kind of unemotional state all the time but that is not true. Angels have emotions, they are just not led by them as they are focused on obedience. Did you also know that angels can change and grow? I have an angel that grows in the spirit as I grow. He has been assigned to me in the financial/business arena. As my gift in that area grows so does his authority. I'm not sure exactly how that works but as I continue to partner with God in this area, I find that my angel is activated in ways it couldn't be otherwise. It is possibly connected to us operating in our authority on earth and the more we are operating in God's plan in the earth the more they can engage with us and help us accomplish whatever assignment we have to fulfill.

Sometimes angels are assigned to us when we step into a place of prayer. I had an angel assigned to me last year when I was in a season of protracted prayer. I had been birthing a fresh revival spirit in my heart and during that time of nightly prayer, I began to see a massive angel show up. Now, this could stretch some of you a bit, but he looked a bit like a fire dragon. I had never seen one before and of course, wanted to make sure he was on my side. As I did some research, I found out that the seraphim in Scripture are also known or referred to in the Hebrew language as a 'fiery serpent'. A bit of a stretch for my normal pictures of the angelic but this angel started showing up regularly as I prayed along with others for a move of God. The Lord gave me a picture of the movie "Avatar". In the movie, there was a giant dragon creature that looked like fire; seemingly untamable. The main character in the movie finds a way to tame him, which preceded him being able to lead the entire avatar army.

We continued to pray for forty-two nights, and during that time it became clear that the angel was assigned to me. I asked some of the other prophets and intercessors there if they saw him and what they thought of him. Their feelings were the same. A powerful part of the army of the Lord. I have seen the 'fire dragon' angel show up at other times. The Lord made it clear that he could only be released at the right time. He didn't specify when that time would be but when I have felt that level of power I have to make sure I check in with God and if I feel his release I begin to release revival fire prayers and preaching and proclamations. Whenever that angel is around and I begin to release that power, the fire is much more tangible to all those in the meeting or event during that time.

WHAT DRAWS AN ANGELS ATTENTION?

If you want to be the kind of person that draws more angelic activity, stay in a place of worship, prayer, obedience, and pursuit of the Kingdom. It's that simple. There is nothing more pleasurable than doing the will of the Father. Too many times to count, when I have been praying or worshipping, angels will show up. As I've said before, I make it a point to acknowledge them, even if I am still worshipping and praying. I reach for them if I can touch them. I lean into them, whatever it takes to step into a proactive approach to their presence.

You may think I'm a bit crazy paying so much attention to the angels but I believe this is part of true Biblical Christianity. Peter engaged the angel that took his chains off and helped him escape prison. Paul was ministered to by an angel who gave him specific instructions for his travels. Jesus was ministered to by angels and said He could call and have His Father send Him a multitude of angels to be at His disposal. Elisha was very aware of the angels and it made him confident in what he was called to do. Elisha had been taught by Elijah who was caught up in the chariot of fire and angelic hosts. Elijah was also comfortable with interacting with angels who he received sustenance from numerous times. Ishmael would have died had his mother not listened to the angel who showed her where the water was to quench their thirst. David waited until he heard the sound of the winds in the trees which marked it was time to go fight for the Lord, Who would give them victory; he was partnering with the angelic.

SUDDENLY AWAKENED BY AN ANGEL

Have you ever been woken up in the middle of the night out of a sound sleep suddenly aware of a presence near your bed? It can be a bit scary. I remember times where I have felt that a sudden and strong presence showing up in my bedroom in the middle of the night. Other times I have felt an awareness of a powerful angel standing in my doorway. If an angel is by my bed and I can't get back to sleep after waking up, I will eventually get up and go downstairs to pray. Sometimes laying in bed and praying is not enough for them as they will not leave me alone until I get up to pray and find out why they are there. After some time in prayer, God will impress something on my heart to go after in targeted prayer. I find that it's not always easy to discern right away, but because I am hungry for the Kingdom to come, breakthroughs to happen, and His secrets to be known, I will simply press in longer. He is a good steward and desires to reveal those treasures to those who are willing to give all to follow Him. Going downstairs after being awakened is one example of responding to the activity of angels.

Some angels carry greater manifested authority than other angels. I think the reason some carry greater manifest authority is it helps convey the message that they were sent with. I know I pay much stronger attention when I feel a higher level of authority resonating off an angel.

PAY ATTENTION TO WHEN THE ANGEL SHOWS UP

There was another time when I was talking on the phone and an angel showed up, during a particular part of the conversation. I have learned in those moments to pay attention to what was just said. In this particular phone call, I happened to be talking to another prophet about humility in an area of his life. When this powerful angel showed up I could feel the fear of the Lord and a scripture reference immediately popped into my head. (This is an example of a more powerful manifest presence showing up with an angel.) As I continued talking, I went and looked up the verse which was found in the book of Daniel. It was the passage where Daniel was exhorting Nebuchadnezzar to be humble and by doing so he would end up being spared the chastisement for what he had been doing wrong. I communicated that verse to my friend and the fear of the Lord hit us both. I went to my knees as I communicated to the other prophet the warning of the Lord to him. It was clear that this angel was there to release a strong warning. The fear of the Lord was needed at this moment. Humility was needed. My prophet friend responded to the encounter with the angel and received the needed change of heart to stay on course.

Sometimes God is so gracious that even when we are not really listening He still sends His angels to help us out of a bind. Genesis 19:15-16 says,

"With the coming of dawn, the angels urged Lot, saying, "Hurry! Take your wife and your two daughters who are here, or you will be swept away when the city is punished. When he hesitated, the men grasped his hand and the hands of his wife and of his two daughters and led them safely out of the city, for the LORD was merciful to them."

We see here that Lot was hesitant to respond to the word that the angels had brought, but God was still merciful to them. God didn't want to destroy them with the rest of the people because of the prayers of Abraham. Learning to respond to the nudges of the Lord through the angelic is important for our protection and advancement of Kingdom assignments.

Consider also Joseph, the Father of Jesus and husband of Mary. He was given an angelic warning in a dream which saved Jesus' life. Sometimes we tend to downplay our dreams and the conversations within them because thinking that God speaks another way. It's a good thing that Joseph took the dream and it's message seriously as the Lord Himself communicating to him about the safety of Mary and Joseph!

ANGELS COME IN DREAMS

I've had a number of dreams where I received an impartation, a word, a revelation, a song, etc. I remember one night dreaming that I was listening to Georgian Banov play his violin when suddenly I got an impartation of his ability to play and bring breakthrough in the spirit. I caught in my dream the spirit of breakthrough through music. So when I woke up, I immediately went to my piano and began playing what I'd heard in my dream. It wasn't a certain song; it was a particular way of playing. I played with precision and authority until breakthrough occurred and since then, have carried that same breakthrough in certain songs that I continue to play on the piano.

Regardless of what form the activity of angels is, whether, in dreams, spiritual form, physical form, with a sense, or a strong sighting, learning how to partner effectively with them is the key. I am not worried about how He wants to come, I just want Him to come. I don't care how I hear from God and His angelic help, I just want to hear from Him and from them. I enjoy going on the adventure of discovering the many different ways that God speaks and am aware of and sensitive to the many different ways that the angels are trying to get our attention.

Questions to Ponder

1. Have you seen any strange looking angels? What did you make of them? What was their assignment?

2. What did you think of Keith's 'Fiery Dragon Angel' story? Do you think this could be Biblical? Why or why not?

3. What are some ways that you can see angel activity increase around you?

4. Have you ever had an angelic encounter where you were hit by the fear of the Lord?

CHAPTER TEN

TESTING THE ANGELIC REALM

I have shared about a deceptive encounter or two I've had in previous chapters. One thing I've learned about these kinds of encounters is that they can happen to anyone. It doesn't mean there's something wrong with you either. Satan can mask himself as an angel of light and so, while we don't need to be afraid of being deceived, we need to be aware of how he does that.

It's pretty simple. Pay attention. Galatians 1:8 says, *"But even if we or an angel from heaven should preach a gospel other than the one we preached to you, let him be eternally condemned!"* Paul speaks here about the possibility of being deceived by an angel. If he shared it, then you know it is possible. Of course, we can always trust that our Father is good and He would never lead us into deception, but we also have a responsibility to know the gospel, stay in community, have people speak into our lives, etc. all of which will help us avoid the possibility of being deceived!

DISCERNING GOOD OR BAD ANGELS

I went through an interesting dynamic recently where for a while I would see an angel show up and then hear a scripture verse or a particular word. One verse spoke of turning 'joy into mourning'. That may not sound like a problem; however, I am in a New Covenant dispensation. In the New Covenant, He turns 'mourning into joy'. I'm not saying there aren't appropriate times of sorrow, but these verses just didn't seem right. Some of the words spoken to me were single words such as "duplicity" or "obsession". Often times I will hear a word in my spirit about the current spiritual giant that a church, a region, or even myself are facing. I have no problem with God giving words that convict and reveal where hearts need to turn towards Him, but when it seems like everything you are hearing from the angelic realm is negative, it's time to test it.

The deceptive angel showed up again right in the middle of an emerging prophet master class I was doing. Since I always welcome the angels when they come, I asked this angel what he wanted to give me. Immediately in my spirit, I heard the verse 'Amos 8:10'. I stopped the online class for just a moment to read the verse and see what he had to say. I wanted to check first to see if what I was picking up in the spirit realm was even worth mentioning or not. It wasn't. It actually tried to take me off track because it was a verse about judgment and weeping. Like I said before, there is a time for that and the Holy Spirit is really great at convicting us when we need an upgrade, but when He initiates it, it is always filled with hope.

I decided that day that enough was enough. This wasn't a good angel. For weeks now I'd been hearing nothing but negativity coming my way. Something I was doing wrong, or something wrong that was going to happen. I just quietly rebuked the angel and then another angel showed up on my right side. I saw in the spirit a small diploma like paper saying, "You've passed." I knew in my spirit that I had been in a test with this false angel. Was I going to receive everything that came to me in the spirit realm or would I test to discern what is good, and avoid all else. God sent an angel to tell me I had passed the test. What a joy!

STAYING ON TRACK

There are a number of things I use to stay on track and be vigilant as I protect my spiritual climate. Firstly, I make sure all things are scriptural. I love it when the Lord reveals a revelation that is not necessarily obvious in those rhema moments. But there are times when God is speaking through a scripture, perhaps out of context, but absolutely biblical and you never build a theology from that place that is anti-Christ or anti-biblical. During those times, I have the wisdom to share with trusted people when I feel a revelation is not literally what the passage is speaking about.

For instance, there is a scripture in Zechariah that, while I have taken it a bit out of context, it still brought some encouragement to me about God's heart. Zechariah 7:9 says, *"This is what the LORD Almighty says: 'Administer true justice; show mercy and compassion to one another."* This passage speaks about justice. God spoke to me that, in the Kingdom, *true* justice is mercy. That is very different than our system of justice. In our Western judicial system, when people commit a crime and hurt others, justice looks like giving the criminal the punishment he deserves. In the Kingdom of God, we don't get what *we* deserve, we get what God deserves. Jesus took our sin and paid the price for it so that we would receive true Kingdom justice, which is mercy. Some would argue that biblical justice is people paying an 'eye for an eye and a tooth for a tooth'. That was Old Covenant justice. In the New

Covenant, people receive mercy. Here's where you can see how differing conclusions could be gained from the passage above in Zechariah. Some could argue what true justice really is. Since we live in the New Covenant, and we've received what Christ deserved, even though this scripture is in the Old Testament where justice looked like an 'eye for an eye', we can conclude that true justice is mercy. We must test everything according to Scripture, but also from a New Covenant lens.

PAY ATTENTION TO LANGUAGE

Another key to testing the angelic is to pay attention to their language. Are they slandering someone? Is what they're communicating building up or tearing down? While many people have success in testing the angelic by simply asking if they are of Jesus Christ, sometimes it's not so easy. Demons that deceive are not always easily figured out as they can appear as an angel of light. They appear good. They seem good. They may even use Scripture, but so did Satan, when he tempted Jesus in the wilderness. What you can look for is their language, their fruit, the heart of what they're saying. I once heard a prophet talk about how his angel would call certain things "stupid" that he felt were being done wrong in the Kingdom. That kind of comment shows me a critical heart and most likely that angel wasn't a good one. Would an angel from God berate something or call it names? I think not. Jude says that even the archangel Michael didn't slander the Devil. Jude 8-10 says,

> *"In the very same way, these dreamers pollute their own bodies, reject authority and slander celestial beings. But even the archangel Michael, when he was disputing with the devil about the body of Moses, did not dare to bring a slanderous accusation against him, but said, "The Lord rebuke you!" Yet these men*

speak abusively against whatever they do not understand; and what things they do understand by instinct, like unreasoning animals—these are the very things that destroy them."

TEST THE ANGELS FRUIT

You can also discern whether the angelic encounter is from God by looking at the fruit. What is the fruit we are looking for? Look for the revelation to draw you closer to God, to help you love people more, and to bring hope and not fear. Hebrews 5:14 admonishes us to be mature and trained in distinguishing good from evil. Are you mature? Can you discern good and evil? How do you do that? You test out the spiritual content coming to you by its fruit. You test it out through Scripture and the nature of God. Pay attention to what is being carried on the language you're hearing, not just the words. A conversation is always happening. We are hearing things from God, the world, the devil, and our own minds, so simply stay in tune with Holy Spirit.

Another safeguard, or key, in discerning the source of the angelic encounter is whether it leaves you wanting to worship the Lord more. The angels that serve the Lord are there to help draw us closer to God, not away from Him, and certainly not to worship *them*.

Revelation 19:10 says,

"At this, I fell at his feet to worship him. But he said to me, "Do not do it! I am a fellow servant with you and with your brothers who hold to the testimony of Jesus. Worship God! For the testimony of Jesus is the spirit of prophecy."

If these encounters don't lead us to Him, they will lead us to a path outside of Him. The original attack by Satan in the garden was to get Adam and Eve to partake of the tree of the knowledge of good and evil. What was that tree? That tree gave them knowledge outside of a relationship with God. Genesis 3:5-7,

> *"For God knows that when you eat of it your eyes will be opened, and you will be like God, knowing good and evil." When the woman saw that the fruit of the tree was good for food and pleasing to the eye, and also desirable for gaining wisdom, she took some and ate it. She also gave some to her husband, who was with her, and he ate it. Then the eyes of both of them were opened, and they realized they were naked; so they sewed fig leaves together and made coverings for themselves."*

The enemy wants us to get spiritual information outside of knowing the source of that information, Jesus Christ. The new age spirit is a spirit that says that everything you need comes from within yourself, that all knowledge can be found within or without, but not from God. That spirit says *you* are God. You are meant to discern good and evil. No, I am meant to trust in the Spirit of God who helps me discern good and evil. I am not meant to pursue knowledge to get wiser, I am meant to pursue God who will make me wiser in the pursuit of Him. Do you see the difference? There are a lot of people out there who have made a fortune by eating of the tree of knowledge of good and evil. They have found a piece of information that is a spiritual principle that works. I have seen people make millions and then boast that it was their hard work. Hard work is a key but it is God who gives the power to create wealth. It just seems like a small tweak to give God the glory for the work that man is doing but it is the difference between eating of the tree of life and the tree of knowledge of good and evil. God is always our source. Anything that is a substitute will become a god and a snare to our true relationship with God.

WATCH OUT FOR ISOLATION

The last key I want to share with you is this. If you start being drawn away from people, the Body of Christ, and healthy interactions with overseers, fathers, and mentors, you are in danger of deception. I have seen many prophetic people begin to pull away from the Body of Christ. They stop asking for advice and input. They begin to receive revelation by themselves alone. That is dangerous and will always cause you to be misguided. I've heard it said by Kris Vallotton that the nature of deception is you don't know you are being deceived. So in order to get out of deception, you have to trust someone more than you trust yourself.

It took me years to learn to trust people more than myself. I was suspicious by nature and had to learn to trust that God had put mentors, my spouse, and others into my life to help me grow. I didn't trust because I was afraid, afraid of being vulnerable out of fear of being punished and judged. I am so thankful that God freed me up of many of those fears. I'm still growing in the area of trust with others, as we all should be; greater trust in God and with others. It is a great path we are on. Proverbs 3:5-6 says,

> "Trust in the LORD with all your heart and lean not on your own understanding; in all your ways acknowledge Him, and He will make your paths straight."

I did a study once on this passage and it read something like this. Trust in the Lord with all your heart and lean not on your own understanding of how I do spiritual things. True trust means we don't always get what God is doing, but we trust Him, friends, and fathers to go the right direction. When we are walking in this trusting place we can be excited about the angelic encounters God has in store for us and can walk in confidence that we will not be led astray.

I pray right now that you would receive an upgrade of the discerning of spirits and that you would mature so that you can truly discern the difference between good and evil. May your eyes be opened to receive the spirit of wisdom and revelation from Heaven so that you can be drawn into a greater relationship with Jesus. Amen.

Questions to Ponder

1. Is the spiritual revelation you're getting causing your heart to be endeared to the Body of Christ or drawn away?

2. Are the encounters you're having causing you to love people better, be more patient, have more trust for others, or do those encounters cause you to draw back from relationships, live in suspicion of others, hold back your affections in relationships?

3. Do the things you receive from the angelic realm concerning the Word build you up or tear you down, draw you closer to God's love or make you feel more condemned?

CHAPTER ELEVEN

ANGELS THAT HELP US

We already know that angels can come into our space. But did you know that they can also pursue us? Isn't that awesome? Look at this verse in Zechariah 4:1, *"Then the angel who talked with me returned and wakened me, as a man is wakened from his sleep. He asked me, 'What do you see?'"* This angel is actually provoking Zechariah and inviting him into a discussion of the supernatural realm. It isn't just for us to pursue the angelic realm, they can actually pursue us. God is so good that He brings the angels to us even if we have no idea about them.

Sometimes we also receive refreshing through angelic help. As I shared in an earlier part of the book, Heather and I were worn out from religious resistance after leading worship for 13 sessions. But the last night God met us with an angelic encounter and we found that our strength and love was returned to us anew. I'm so thankful that even in our weariness, He is pursuing us to bring what we need most. Many times, that pursuit involves Him sending angels to minister to us. Look at Psalm 91:11-12,

> *"For He will command His angels concerning you to guard you in all your ways; they will lift you up in their hands so that you will not strike your foot against a stone."*

And at Psalm 91:14,

> *"Because he loves Me," says the LORD, "I will rescue him; I will protect him, for he acknowledges My name."*

Of course, He pursued us *first*! As John 3:16 says, He was the one Who loved the world first. I'm writing this to help us realize it is still by grace that we get to encounter the supernatural realm that God has designed for us to enjoy and encounter. He is the one that has given us grace and mercy to come to Him at any time. It is His gift to us.

There are so many times when we are off-kilter, discouraged, weary, etc. but God is still faithful to pursue us with His provision for what is needed. Remember when Elijah was running from Jezebel in fear in I Kings 19:3-6?

> *"Elijah was afraid and ran for his life. When he came to Beersheba in Judah, he left his servant there, while he himself went a day's journey into the desert. He came to a broom tree, sat down under it and prayed that he might die. "I have had enough, LORD," he said. "Take my life; I am no better than my ancestors." Then he lay down under the tree and fell asleep. All at once an angel touched him and said, "Get up and eat." He looked around, and there by his head was a cake of bread baked over hot coals, and a jar of water. He ate and drank and then lay down again."*

Elijah is fleeing for his life. He tells the Lord he has had enough. He doesn't want to go on. What does God do? He sends him an angel with food so that he can go on. God doesn't answer Elijah's prayer or even treat him according to his weakness at this moment but according to His graciousness as a father to his son. Elijah needed to be loved on. God really is that good.

ANGELS WANT ME TO OBEY

I've had times where I wanted to disobey. I've been worn down by life and the constant battle of choosing to do the right thing. I've thought before that, maybe the wrong thing to do in my life is actually the right thing. I've wanted to give up on meaningful relationships and ministry. It was in these moments that God would graciously say, '*Son if you keep going down this path, it isn't going to end well.*' When He speaks, He empowers the listener to turn back in the right direction. He's always helped me get back on the right course.

I love the story in Daniel Chapter 10, it is a great example of angelic help. Daniel is at a moment of weakness when he is met by an angel. Daniel 10:15-19,

> "*While he was saying this to me, I bowed with my face toward the ground and was speechless. Then one who looked like a man touched my lips, and I opened my mouth and began to speak. I said to the one standing before me, "I am overcome with anguish because of the vision, my lord, and I am helpless. How can I, your servant, talk with you, my lord? My strength is gone and I can hardly breathe." Again the one who looked like a man touched me and gave me strength. "Do not be afraid, O man highly esteemed," he said. "Peace! Be strong now; be strong." When he spoke to me, I was strengthened and said, 'Speak, my lord, since you have given me strength.'"*

We all need outside help. Even the other day I was tired and needing encouragement when suddenly I became aware of an angel near me. I felt my head immediately get warm and great peace. That was an angel ministering to me when I needed it!

UNDERSTANDING THE PRIORITY OF GOD OVER ANGELS

I think it's important in a book about angels to understand that, while we can learn the art of attracting angels and partnering with them, it doesn't happen outside of God's help. It's still a gift from Him. Some people have always had the ability to see the angelic realm. They didn't earn it, nor do we. Being able to connect with God and the realm of the spirit is a gift. He is our Dad and He is supernatural. In that realm there are angels. As we are in pursuit of Him and His Kingdom, He entrusts us with angels that rescue, protect, and keep us on the right course.

I shared this story in a previous Chapter, but look again at Lot who didn't want to leave Sodom. God in His mercy had the angels continue to be patient with him, probably because of the prayers of Abraham. Genesis 19:16 says,

> "When he hesitated, the men grasped his hand and the hands of his wife and of his two daughters and led them safely out of the city, for the LORD was merciful to them."

I'm so glad we have angelic help even when we are not cooperating with God, running away from Him like Balaam, or not facing our problems out of fear like Elijah. God is so patient with every one of us. It's amazing that the angels can have patience, though I suspect they are patient because the Lord is patient.

The bottom line is, angels are on assignment and we are not in charge. They are there to honor God and carry out His assignments. It doesn't mean they can't endure resistance or don't have a struggle to fight through, like in Daniel 10 where the angel took three weeks to bring the answer to Daniel's prayer, but it does mean they won't stop until they accomplish what God assigned them to do.

I am so thankful that God is on our side and has given us every victory. He sends angels to ensure that we get to our destiny. Sometimes they come when we are disobeying, other times they come when we are weak, other times they come when we are praying, and other times they come when we are not even seeking help. God is faithful and will give us what we need to win. Angels carry the gifts to get us there. Let's have an expectation that God is releasing angels on our behalf on a regular basis to help us, serve us, and keep us going in the right direction.

Let's posture ourselves in a position of receptivity and say, *"Lord I'm here right now receiving from Your grace, receiving the angelic help, receiving mercy for what is needed right now. Thanks, heavenly Dad that it is not all about me and that sometimes You are pursuing me and sending Your angels to help me get where I don't even know I should be. Amen!"*

Questions to Ponder

1. Have you ever had an angel show up to help you in a time of need? What did that look like?

2. Have you ever been discouraged and then felt the presence of God come on you? Did you recognize that it was the angel from the Lord ministering to you?

3. What do you think you could do to increase sensitivity to angels that are wanting to partner and minister to and with you?

… CHAPTER TWELVE …

DIFFERING AUTHORITY IN THE ANGELIC

Angels carry different levels of authority according to their assignments. Some angels have a much greater sphere than others because of the realm they're assigned to. God decides their sphere and entrusts us with encountering the differing levels of angelic authority according to our sphere. Depending on your metron, or realm of influence, you may not experience angels that are over regions, nations, or larger geographic realms. Of course, you could experience an angelic encounter within the sphere you live if you're a part of the Kingdom solution to that region.

A few of the stories I've shared in this book bear mentioning again. Fairly recently, I met the angel of awakening. All I could see of him in the hotel room were his feet and the bottom part of his legs but he was absolutely massive. While I have sensed angels of awakening with me at other times, they were different and were not as big. There could be several angels with similar assignments but one who carries a greater metron of influence than another, thus the size difference.

THE ANGEL CALLED SANDY

I have also seen an angel named 'Sandy', which is also massive in size. I have seen this angel show up when recurring disasters happened in America. The angel named 'Sandy' was no small ranking angel. There was Hurricane Sandy, the deadly shootings at Sandy Hook High school, to name a couple. At one point, an angel showed up and the Lord spoke to me that Sandy was the name of the angel. So I did a study and realized the name meant, 'defender of mankind'. It was so strange that the name Sandy was connected to these disasters when the meaning was quite the opposite. I even saw in Scripture a reference to this 'Sandy anointing' found in Psalm 68:5. We see in this verse God's heart to be our defender, *"A father to the fatherless, a defender of widows, is God in His holy dwelling."* I realized that I needed to begin to pray to partner with this angel for our nation that protection would come and that God would defend us against the enemy that seeks to devour. The angel wasn't there to bring disaster but to ward off disaster, but the angel needed our partnership to avert the disasters or to greatly diminish the destruction caused by natural disasters.

Many times we see in Scripture when there is a battle over a nation, there are also high ranking angels present. Daniel 10:12-14 says,

> *"Then he continued, "Do not be afraid, Daniel. Since the first day that you set your mind to gain understanding and to humble yourself before your God, your words were heard, and*

I have come in response to them. But the prince of the Persian kingdom resisted me twenty-one days. Then Michael, one of the chief princes, came to help me because I was detained there with the king of Persia. Now I have come to explain to you what will happen to your people in the future, for the vision concerns a time yet to come."

Daniel's prayers unleashed the help of powerful angelic help. Michael the archangel came to the rescue but even then it still took three weeks. This shows us the power of our prayers in releasing the kind of help that we need. Sometimes we think that angels are just sovereignly released and we have no sway in their movements. But the truth is they are waiting to partner with us, as we partner with God in obedience to what He calls us to do.

We see in the life of several of the Apostles during a time of persecution when they needed angelic help. James had been caught by Herod and killed. Then he caught Peter and decide to do the same thing to him but something else happens as we see in Acts 12:1-5,

"It was about this time that King Herod arrested some who belonged to the church, intending to persecute them. He had James, the brother of John, put to death with the sword. When he saw that this pleased the Jews, he proceeded to seize Peter also. This happened during the Feast of Unleavened Bread. After arresting him, he put him in prison, handing him over to be guarded by four squads of four soldiers each. Herod intended to bring him out for public trial after the Passover. So Peter was kept in prison, but the church was earnestly praying to God for him."

PRAYER DOES BRING ANGELS

What was the shift that released the angelic help? It was prayer. It wasn't some random thing where God decided to save Peter but not James. No the outcome of both of the Apostles' lives were in the hands of praying saints. What if the release of the type of angels we need is, at times, in direct proportion to our prayers? Some saints look on with devastation as the nation's fail, disasters occur, and people's lives are destroyed. Other saints see the same devastation but realize that we are called to partner with heaven to see those things changed through prayer.

Was James' death the will of God? Was Peter's life being saved the will of God? Maybe the will of God was found in both. The saints didn't pray and so James became a martyr. This is still an amazing finish to his race; there is a reward for this kind of death. Remember Apostle Paul said that he was willing and ready to go to his death. The saints wanted him not to go but he was ready. Which was right? What Paul decided. With Peter, the saints prayed and Peter's life was miraculously saved. That is also the will of God. What if we started praying when we saw things that were not right? What kind of help would be released in the angelic? Or what if we started praying for those people who seem like they'll never change?

I remember a close loved one not walking with God and looking like they never would. I heard the Lord whisper into my spirit that they would only be brought into the Kingdom if someone fought for them in prayer. I did a piece of that fighting and I know that others did too. Now, that dear loved one had a miraculous turnaround and fully serves the Lord. I love to pray and agree with God and the angels, through prayer for all kinds of breakthroughs here on earth.

IT'S NICE WHEN ANGELS COME QUICKLY

Other battles seem to yield much easier than others. Another time when Daniel prayed, an angel was immediately released. In fact, even when he was still *in* prayer the answer was released. Praise the Lord when the battle is that easy. Prayer goes up and an angel comes down. In this case, the angel that came down was another archangel, Gabriel. Not bad for one prayer.

Even Jesus Himself prayed and had angelic help released on his behalf. Jesus was in the throes of death about to go to the cross and wrestling with the weight of the world's sin, the devil, and His faltering disciples. In the midst of this, He prays to gain strength. This is God in the flesh. He didn't use the power that He could have used from heaven to save Himself, but showed us how to pray, to lean on God for strength, and to do what we're assigned to do. When He prayed, angels were sent to strengthen Him.

SOMETIMES TURNING TO GOD IS ALL THAT IS NEEDED

Sometimes partnering with angels is not so much about touching them, knowing where they are, seeing them, feeling them, all the things that we have talked about. Sometimes partnering with the angelic is found in simply turning your heart to heaven and saying God I need your help and guidance. When we do that, angels come to bring the help that is needed. Have you ever prayed but it just feels like you're getting nowhere? I have many times. There have been seasons where I have prayed and I have wept. I have cried and I have warred in the heavens. There have been times where I have pounded the bed that I knelt by and said God I must have a breakthrough. It is in those desperate times that our resolve for the things of God gets stronger. But it is also in those times that God is delighted to send His angelic help for the level of breakthrough that we are wrestling for.

May you be one of the ones that angels love to be around because you have chosen to pursue Him and His Kingdom at all costs. May you also be a person of prayer that causes the angelic realm to war on your behalf as they are released to help you from your heavenly Father. I love what Jesus said in Matthew 26:53, *"Do you think I cannot call on my Father, and He will at once put at My disposal more than twelve legions of angels?"* God's heart is to send His angels to help us, according to the level of breakthrough we need and there are specific angels for those breakthroughs.

Questions to Ponder

1. What are the spheres of authority that you are assigned to?

2. Have you noticed any angels that carry authority for your city, region, or nation?

3. What have you done to partner with those angels?

4. Are there times where you have noticed that an angel came after you had been praying?

5. What did that teach you about prayer?

CHAPTER THIRTEEN

PARTNERING WITH THE ANGELIC UNLEASHES PROVISION

A few years ago, I had a prophecy given to me that encouraged Heather and me that we would begin to learn how to operate with angelic hosts. They also said that the eyes of God were coming on us, were all around us, and that meant God's favor was coming. Not long after that, I was in another city to minister at a church. I had been picked up by two completely new connections. One of the guys was a businessman and the other guy was a vocational minister of a local church. I hadn't met them before and frankly wasn't really in the mood to engage much in much chit-chat as I had a bad headache and was focused on the meeting later that night.

MINISTERING WITH A HEADACHE

I just love it when God calls on you to minister even when you're not in a great frame of mind; this was certainly one of those nights. I was sitting in the back of the car when suddenly I saw an eye in the sky. As strange as that sounds, it was clear as a bell in my vision. Then I remembered the word for Heather and me that the eyes of God would be on us. I had done some research about eyes in the Bible and had some insights from my study of the encounter that Abraham had with Isaac when he went to sacrifice him on the mountain. The King James translation says in Genesis 22:14, *"And Abraham called the name of that place Jehovahjireh: as it is said to this day, in the mount of the LORD it shall be seen."* God had already been showing me that part of the eyes appearing and being on us was actually about *provision*. Abraham needed provision and instead of sacrificing his son, God showed him a ram.

So here I was with two people I was meeting for the first time, not in the mood necessarily to minister, but God reminded me about His promise of provision through an 'eye in the sky'. Not wanting to miss my window of opportunity to partner with what God was doing, I responded. I began to prophesy over the people who sat in the front seats of the car. I didn't know much at all about them. But as I ministered to them clarity and breakthrough began to come to both of them. One of them, the businessman, reached out to me because of that and began to sow into my ministry on a regular basis. He became a significant source of finances that took me through a very lean season. I would have missed that resource for the Lord's provision had I not paid attention to an eye in the sky.

ANGELS HELP WITH PROVISION

Angels are a part of bringing provision. We already saw that in the story about Elijah when angels brought him food and water for his journey.

Another story in Genesis speaks about this same kind of provision for Ishmael and Hagar through the angelic. Genesis 21:17-19,

> "God heard the boy crying, and the angel of God called to Hagar from heaven and said to her, "What is the matter, Hagar? Do not be afraid; God has heard the boy crying as he lies there. Lift the boy up and take him by the hand, for I will make him into a great nation. Then God opened her eyes and she saw a well of water. So she went and filled the skin with water and gave the boy a drink."

We also see an angel of the Lord calling from heaven to stop Abraham from sacrificing Isaac in Genesis 22:10-11. After stopping Abraham, the angel showed Abraham where the provision (ram) was. There is a definite partnership between God and the angels that we can see in these stories. Even if an angel isn't mentioned, it doesn't mean they weren't used. It can also be assumed that if an angel is present in a story, that God was the author of that angelic help as well.

Many times, I have encountered the angels of provision. Ultimately, provision comes from heaven through Christ according to Philippians 4:19, "*But my God shall supply all your needs according to His riches in glory by Christ Jesus.*" God is providing for us and there is provision for everything that is needed in life but it is found in the relationship with God. God distributes those provisions through the angels that help!

Psalm 78:24-25,

> "*He rained down manna for the people to eat, He gave them the grain of heaven. Men ate the bread of angels; He sent them all the food they could eat.*"

Wow, this is amazing. There was food raining down from heaven on a continual basis, day after day, year after year. This was the food of angels.

Was it provided daily by the angels? I don't know. But what I do know is that angels provide food and we need to learn to expect their help in receiving provision for food, clothing, and even protection. I have witnessed many times where something harmful should have happened to me or others and God protected me, and hardly a scratch happened where certain death should have been the outcome. Psalm 91:11-12 says,

> *"For He will command His angels concerning you to guard you in all your ways; they will lift you up in their hands so that you will not strike your foot against a stone."*

The angels' job is to protect God's loved ones. Some may ask why some people still die, yet another life was preserved. I certainly won't presume to know those answers but I do know that God promises protection and angels are agents of that protection. I regularly pray Psalm 91 over my family. I ask for the Father to send His angels to protect their coming and going. That is the provision of God as well, protection.

I also believe that praying a simple prayer of thanks for our food released protection, as I Timothy 4:4-5 says. The word and prayer consecrate our food. Prayer invites the angelic to come. Who knows what they are doing when we are praying over our food but maybe they are removing toxins and things that should not be.

Regardless of how the provision comes and what form it comes in, how wonderful of a Father we have to provide it for us through so many wonderful ways. I am so grateful for the angels who bring provision!

Questions to Ponder

1. Have you ever seen supernatural provision come to you?

2. How did it come?

3. How did you know that it was supernatural?

4. Was there ever a time where you know angels were apart of a miracle of provision for you? How did you know that?

5. What did you learn about the angels in these interactions?

CHAPTER FOURTEEN

ANGELS HONOR GOD'S VALUES

When God's angels show up, it is important that we have the right posture around them. The posture is not one of worship but one of honor and respect. The angels don't want to be worshiped but they do require respect. How do we respect them? By honoring the word of the Lord and the assignment they are carrying. When they bring a word, even if it is correctional, it is for our benefit and being humble to receive it and make whatever adjustments are needed is the right response.

So many people in the Bible had the opposite response and it never ended well. Nebuchadnezzar did not repent by humbling himself and being kind to the poor and it wasn't too long before he was crawling around like an animal for seven years. Nebuchadnezzar was given the opportunity to avoid this level of discipline, had he listened to the angelic messenger that spoke to him in a dream. God's heart is always for our benefit and He is so compassionate and patient when we respond to Him appropriately.

PAYING ATTENTION TO THE ANGELS WILL CERTAINLY HELP YOU

Balaam was another example of not honoring the message that came through an angel. Number 22:22-23 says, *"But God was very angry when he (Balaam) went, and the angel of the LORD stood in the road to oppose him. When the donkey saw the angel of the LORD standing in the road with a drawn sword in his hand, she turned off the road into a field. Balaam beat her to get her back on the road."* One of the things that angels bring to our world is the fear of the Lord. Angels stand in the presence of the Lord and so they carry the presence of the Lord. When Balaam's donkey saw the angel of the Lord, the donkey turned aside in fear when Balaam didn't. There are certain angels that are very nice and patient. They are even gracious like the angel that met Balaam, despite his disobedient heart. Balaam's problem was that he continually chose to do something that God didn't want, even after this angelic encounter and a talking donkey! Of course, we know the final outcome of Balaam's continual testing of God was that he was killed in the end. Not the story I want.

I have spoken into many peoples' lives when they are not walking in obedience to God and even seen an angel show up to bring a message of repentance to them. God in His loving way is always trying to give one more chance. And, as I said in an earlier chapter, often times when you see God, an angel is present, and when you see an angel, God is present. When Moses had the encounter with an angel in the burning bush, was it an angel or the Lord. It was probably both.

When God brings us warnings, He still loves us and we are still in the New Covenant. When we ignore those warnings, coming from an angel, or God, we disrespect and dishonor God, and the angelic. I have had times in my life where the temptation to sin was there. I felt worn out, discouraged, lonely, tired, and hopeless. The devil knows just when to come and bring temptation. Sometimes I have been tempted to look at something, think about something, say something inappropriate or sinful but all of a sudden I am aware of an angel nearby and that I am not alone. I heard someone say that the angels don't look in while you are doing "private" things. I don't know that to be true. That hasn't been the case for me. It seems like the angels can be very present when you are in private moments. They have been given certain permissions to help you succeed. Sometimes they stand afar and don't interact with you but at other times they do.

In those times of struggle, the fear of the Lord would become very strong. I have heard His voice, seen the angels, and received revelation about the strategy of the enemy. I would feel His love but also feel His heart for me and how what I was tempted to do would hurt Him. Always a loving, kind, but firm Father calling me back to His heart. Not wanting to hurt Him, I would just run back into His arms and find new strength, new grace, and a new day waiting for me to walk victoriously where the enemy was attacking me. God loves that kind of heart. He is super compassionate to those who, even though they have been worn down, they hear from the Lord or have an angelic encounter and return to run towards Him at full force.

ANGELS CAN BRING MANY THINGS

Angels are sent to bring us a word of correction, conviction, and revelation that will set us on the right path. I believe the Lord is releasing this book now because He wants the body of Christ to begin to pay attention to the angelic help He sends. Help comes in many ways. Sometimes help comes in the form of conviction. Sometimes help comes in the form of good discipline. It is so wonderful when you hear His rebuke and turn and follow Him; there is such hope in it. His ways are higher and whenever you respond to Him and turn from whatever you were doing, saying, or thinking, His presence is so rewarding. His angels are there to help us get going down the right path.

I love it when the angels of fire show up. I become inflamed with a passion to honor the Lord at all costs. I burn with holy fire to see the Church step into all she has been destined to step into. My heart grieves with the compromises that so much of the Church is walking in but rejoices when the Church yields. Learning to partner with these angels of fire requires us to walk in the fire with the Lord as well. The fire is God's love and in His love, there is no room for enduring sin. If you say you love God and don't obey His commands, the love of God is not in you I John 3 says.

We want to be the ones that the Father acknowledges before His angels because we lived fully for the Father. Just imagine the Father saying, "*Look at my servant _____ there. They have continually chosen to walk in My ways despite the temptations, trials, discouragement, and testing that they have endured. They have chosen Me along the way. They have fallen a few times but they keep getting up and pursuing Me. I am so pleased with them. Angels, I just want you to know that that person is worth My attention and because I am giving them attention, I give you permission to also give them attention. Help them out. Go serve them. I love them and want to make sure they are well protected, covered, and taken care of.*"

Can't you hear the Father speaking that about you? If you can't hear Him say that now then let the fear of the Lord provoke you to be jealous for it. He wants to acknowledge you before the angels. Look at people like Noah, Daniel, and Job, who captured the Lord's heart by choosing Him when others didn't, when it wasn't popular. But they were popular before God. And they had a lot of supernatural help, angels serving them.

BE THE KIND OF PERSON ANGELS WANT TO HELP

Oh to be the kind of committed believer that the angels can't wait to help and love to hang around with. To be the one that steps out in courage even in the face of fear. To be the one that chooses purity when compromise would be easier. To be the one who prays when betraying would be the easier option. To be the one who loves when hating would be more comforting. To be the one who chooses joy, worship, thanksgiving, and hope when others choose doubt, discouragement, unbelief, and worry. That is what God desires for each of us. He is committed to seeing us get there. His plans are to see us prosper. He is for us and not against us. He has dispatched His angels on our behalf. They are waiting for our partnership. They are waiting for us to pay attention to them. They are waiting for us to honor the Lord.

I cherish too much the approval of the Father, the help of the angelic, the love of Jesus, and the comfort of the Holy Spirit to run into the arms of sin. I am His and He is mine. By His grace, I stand and so can you. I am praying for you that you will step into a season of going from glory to glory, angelic encounter to angelic encounter. I pray that you would have eyes to see what the Spirit is saying and showing you. I pray that you would turn towards the Lord and not resist Him in any way. I pray that you would pay attention when you hear His voice, when you feel those angelic nudges when you begin to hear in your spirit conversations from God and His angels who bring important pieces of revelation that you need to listen to.

God is with you, and so are the angels.

Questions to Ponder

1. Did you catch the heart of the fear of the Lord in this closing chapter?

2. Have you recognized that there are angels that come to keep you walking in God's ways and not into missing the mark Heaven has for you?

3. What can you do to be more intentional about partnering with the angels?

4. What was your favorite chapter in this book? Why?

ABOUT THE AUTHOR

Keith Ferrante is a prophetic voice who travels internationally speaking in churches, conferences, ministry schools, and other venues. Keith carries a message of freedom for the body of Christ helping to bring revival and reformation. He is a prophetic voice that carries a breaker anointing to open up the heavens and brings timely corporate and personal prophetic words. Keith has developed many resources that offer fresh perspective on the prophetic, supernatural Kingdom-character, and spiritual gifting. Keith is passionate to see the fullness of heaven's atmosphere here on earth and brings people into divine reality through joyful glory encounters, impartation, and signs and wonders.

Keith is the founder and director of Emerging Prophets, a ministry that provides resources for highly gifted prophetic individuals. The ministry helps them discover whether or not they are a prophet, what kind of a prophet they are, and resources and lessons that help develop the much-needed character to move from the calling of prophet to the office of prophet. Keith is also a prophetic life consultant assisting highly motivated individuals and influencers achieve breakthrough in their personal and spiritual life, business, and position of influence.

EMERGING PROPHET SCHOOL

If you are interested in developing your prophetic call or discovering if you are a prophet, visit their website at *www.emergingprophets.com* to find out how you can sign up for a module on our online school or attend a regional Emerging Prophet school near you. If you are interested in personally being developed as an emerging prophet, we also offer coaching for developing prophets, as well as marketplace leaders. If you are interested in hosting an Emerging Prophet weekend intensive to introduce the concept of developing prophets in your area, please contact us. Also if you are interested in starting an Emerging Prophet School in your area, we would love to chat with you.

If you would like to host Keith Ferrante or one of the Emerging Prophet trainers to minister in your area, please contact us.

www.emergingprophets.com

MORE RESOURCES FROM KEITH FERRANTE

BOOKS:

- *The Happy Prophet*
- *New Covenant Prophet*
- *Embracing the Emerging Prophets*
- *There must be More*
- *Keys to Abundance*
- *Restoring the Fathers Heart*
- *Reforming the Church from a House to a Home*
- *Emerging Prophets Discovering your Identity Workbook*
- *Emerging Prophets Discovering your Metron Workbook*
- *Emerging Prophets Calling to Office Discovery Workbook*

MUSIC CDs

- Unveiled Mysteries
- Where you are
- New Sounds
- Falling Into You
- Songs from Heaven

These are available at our website:

www.emergingprophets.com

Made in the
USA
Lexington, KY